DON'T MISS IT IF YOU CAN!

DON'T MISS IT IF YOU CAN!

BY JESS MOODY

WORD BOOKS   WACO, TEXAS

There is one kind of laugh that I always did recommend: it looks out of the eye first with a merry twinkle, then it creeps down on its hands and knees and plays around the mouth like a pretty moth around the blaze of a candle, then it steals over into the dimples of the cheeks and rides around into those little whirl-pools for a while, then it lights up the whole face like the mellow bloom of a damask rose, then it swims off on the air with a peal as clear and as happy as a dinner-bell, then it goes back again on golden tiptoe like an angel out for an airing, and lays down on its little bed of violets in the heart where it came from.

—Josh Billings

DEDICATION

TO PAT AND MARTHA, who seem to be disgustingly and disarmingly normal—in spite of the fact that they are "Peekays".
. . .

TO DORIS, a poor preacher's widow . . .

TO JEANNE, my precious sister with the pretty red hair . . .

TO MOTHER MOODY, who at eighty drives seventy-five mph —in reverse—against a one way street—who takes life and romps with it . . .

TO MOM CUMMINS—at least the best person I ever knew . . .

TO DAD MOODY, eminent discoverer of Dr. Moody's health drink . . . . and great teacher in life's most important course: solving the human equation . . .

TO MILTON DUPRIEST, who is kin to everybody . . . . and loves us all . . .

TO JOHN HAGGI, Demosthenes' little brother, eloquent as Apollos . . .

TO ED CLARK, happy combination of Jonathan Winters, The Smothers Brothers, and Francis of Assisi . . .

TO PAUL HARVEY, Ben Hogan's golf teacher and my personal pro . . .

TO THE OLD *SHIELD* MAGAZINE AND "WHERE HE LEADS" GANG . . .

TO JOHN EWING, who carried me through . . .

TO SEBASTIAN PEPOOFNIC, who knows why . . .

TO THE THORNS IN THE FLESH who all during my ministry have kept me on my toes. . . .

TO MRS. R. H. DOBBS, sweet little Jesus girl . . .

. . . . and finally to JESS C. MOODY, of whom Lyndon B. Johnson said, "Who?"

v

A

Aardvark

This is not really about the aardvark, but isn't he the one who starts every alphabetically arranged book? What would it do to his ego if he discovered he was left out of *my* alphabetically arranged book? I don't want to incur the wrath of all the Aardvarks in the world.

This makes it possible for me to begin my book with the story with which I wanted to begin it. You can't discover why I wanted to begin it with this story unless you read the entire volume.

I have a friend, a building contractor, a Mr. Aaron A. Aardvark. He prides himself on constructing perfectly magnificent buildings. Once he was surveying a newly-completed edifice, and he spied one extra brick lying on the ground. He picked it up, not able to imagine how he had so miscalculated his brick order as to have one left over. This was profligacy.

He called one of his workmen, a Mr. O. Bascom Wilhoyte, asking what should be done with the one extra brick.

Wilhoyte responded immediately, "There's only one thing to do, sir. You must throw the brick straight up in the air."

And he did just that.

Abstract Art

A product of the untalented, sold by the unprincipled, to the totally blind, signifying nothing.

It is a fact that a certain work of abstract art won a blue ribbon, and was viewed by more than 100,000 people before a scholar noticed that it was upside down.

Anything that communicates that poorly must be very outstanding.

Most of them appear to be the work of a doddering, senile
epileptic with hiccups.

It seems to be the visual projection of a very interesting case of
the DT's.

Actor

The greatest supporting actor in all history is Tommy Man-
ville.

Dr. W. W. Adams

He has so much grit, he would preach against the brimstone
industry in a city two miles from the gates of hell.

If most ministers dealt with evil as forcefully as does this old
professor from New Orleans Seminary, they would lose their
churches within a month.

Adulthood

When you cease sucking your thumbs and start twiddling
them . . . . a season of stupification.

Affluence

The churches are too rich and comfortable. If the goodness of God doesn't lead us to repentance and zeal, He might subject us to persecution and dispersion.

Historically, this has always been healthy for the churches. O, may He not be required to say, "To your health!"

Air Sickness

Next time
I'll traffic
By National
Geographic
Airsickness is quite an agony but not so bad as airplane poison. One drop will kill you.

Alcoholism

A one way street to nowhere. Ministers stand against liquor, not because they are narrow bigots and prudes; rather because they would like to get some rest from the multiplicities of night calls, some relaxing of the oppressive time consumption to help alleviate the family disintegration due to alcohol.

The journalists or the motion picture industry do not seem to know what is happening behind the scenes—but the simple minister knows.

Steve Allen

As my old friend, Puppy Tail, used to say, "He is a smart genius!"

America

What kind of America are we trying to save? What part of America deserves saving? I have a belief that only a nation that deserves saving can be. What am I doing to make America more worthy of being saved? Until these and other similarly embarrassing questions are answered, we will do little for the national good.

C. Roy Angell

A Miami minister famous for his ability to tell stories. Often Dr. Angell would dramatize his stories punctuating them with gestures. Everything went fine in his church as he preached his great sermons until the day he nearly lost his choir which was convulsed with laughter.

After the service, Dr. Angell inquired as to what was so funny. One of the choir members told him, "Dr. Angell, the members of the choir who sit behind you didn't know how effective a dramatist you were until you told the story about how the little dog wagged his tail as his master came home!"

Anger

Don't be angry at anything but Johnson grass and mosquitoes.

4

Argument

An exchange of glandular venom. Both sides always lose.

Arrival

Disappointment

Arrogancy

A combination of surging ambition and deep insecurity.

Art

That which does not need a PR man to put over. A true artist is a born genius who works 18 hours a day at his task and is over 50 years of age.

Atheism

I note that among other plans, Mrs. Madalyn Murray, the famous atheist of Baltimore, Maryland, who reputedly has made fun of churches for attempting to raise money, is trying to raise money. She plans the establishment of an atheist university, an atheist printing plant, and an atheistic radio station.

But the most interesting of her plans is a home for aged atheists.

What do aged atheists have to talk about as they sit around waiting to die?

Do they discuss the legacy of morality, decency, integrity, and spiritual sensitivity they have bequeathed their children?

Or the good atheism has done the world: the hospitals, orphanages, the elevation of womanhood, and the mass distribution of decent literature?

Perhaps they discuss the great bulwark against Communism their atheism has erected.

Then when the sun is sinking low, and conversation for the wheel chair atheists begins to lull, they can joyously contemplate their future.

There is so much for an aged atheist to look forward to.

Old atheists never die . . .

  . . . they just go to Hell.

Augustine

One of the finest of Augustine's many scintillating statements was, "Let us not despair; one of the thieves was saved. Let us not presume; one of the thieves was lost."

Authority

I have always believed that authorities should be consulted. The right of private interpretation does not mean that one man's ignorance is as accurate as another man's intelligence.

I find people who would never advise a lawyer on how to interpret the law, who couldn't be forced to instruct a physician as to how to perform a lobotomy, can instruct a minister, who has received eleven years of training in his field, about all biblical interpretations and how to administrate a vast church program.

With great love for laymen, I must state that almost without exception, their advice has been based on a fragmentary rather than a whole concept of the church.

Autobiography

The life story of an auto, entitled *"Only 36 More Payments and I'm Junk."*

Automation and the Ministry

Automation will replace nine out of ten working people within the next thirty years.

That's what the man said.

Immediately I was seized with a barely controlled hysteria. Am I finished at thirty nine?

Instead of saying "Whatever happened to the Baby Jane?", will they be saying "Whatever happened to the Baptist Jess?"

I can hear them now. "Oh, he was last seen in Nova Scotia, walking toward the ocean."

Will I be replaced by nuts, bolts, transistors, and wires? I wouldn't dare let my church know my fears about this. There are some pretty frugal boys on that Finance Committee.

I can hear one of them now. He stands before the whole church and reads the advantages of an automated pastor over one who is mere flesh.

"Brethren, there are many reasons why XL-230B-214 should replace Dr. Moody, much as we appreciate the services he has rendered in the past.

"For one thing, we could sell the parsonage. We could store XL-230B-214 in a closet around here somewhere.

"Also, it would put the church completely in the hands of the laymen. Isn't that considered the Baptist Ideal?

"If we have a problem in the church, our Official Button Pusher—elected by democratic action of the congregation—could feed the question into XL-230B-214's mouth, there would be a whirring sound and the southwide approved answer would come out in his hand! We laymen could carry out the work prescribed.

"Additionally, think of the power of his pulpit prayers. We could feed the prayers of John Knox, George Truett, Norman Vincent Peale, even Billy Graham into our new pastor's electronic brain. No more of those routine moody Moody prayers.

"Further consideration should be given to the fact that we can play the sermons we like by the great ministers of the world. If we don't want a sermon on labor-management, alcohol, or the race issue, we don't have to hear it. We can play a tape that plays the pure Gospel, without all these so called implications.

"You might say, 'But the machine costs $60,000!' That's a good amount, but have you considered that XL-230B-214 is guaranteed for twenty years with a maintenance cost of only $1,000 per annum? What pastor have we ever had who was guaranteed for that long and could be maintained for $1,000 a year?

"This brings XL's—I hope you will not be offended by my referring to him by his first letters—I repeat, this brings his average annual cost to only $4,000 per annum, exclusive of tape recorded sermons and prayers, which would amount to only a couple of hundred a year. Think of the saving!"

I shudder to think of the outcome of that particular motion. I'd better shape up; I might be replaced by a button.

Autosuggestion

I pick myself up by the hair, hold myself at arm's length, look myself in the eye, and bark orders at me. As soon as I see that I am not looking, I ignore them.

B

Babies

A howling success. When my boy was two days old he preached his first sermon to the other babies in the hospital. I am not exaggerating one bit when I tell you that when he came to the end of his message there was not a dry seat in the house.

Joe Weldon Bailey

One of those blessed saints who has learned to balance being perfectly natural with intense spirituality.

At a Baptist convention JWB quietly singled out one pastor after another. Then, with a look of deep concern, said, "I'm *so* sorry to hear of the problem you are having in your church."

Invariably, the hasty response was "Wait a minute! You haven't heard my side of the story."

Once JWB sent a flock of telegrams to pastors of all kinds of churches, with the simple message "My congratulations to you."

Nearly everyone of them responded with a note of appreciation to Mr. B. for being aware of the contribution he was making.

Only *one* wrote "For what?"

Bailey was mowing his lawn one afternoon and the janitor dashed up to him to remind him that he was to conduct a wedding at three P.M. and it was now three P.M.

JWB set a record getting properly attired, leaped into his car dashed to the church, ran into the chapel, took his place at the altar.

He was quite pleased that everything had worked out without incident.

9

While warmly purring within that all was well and waiting for the lovely bride to glide to the altar, he noticed a bewildered look on the faces of many in the congregation.

They were gazing at his feet.

He looked down.

His lovely feet were attired . . .

      . . . with tennis shoes.

The purring ceased.

Baldness

When a man is forty, his hair starts growing inwardly. If it strikes gray matter, it comes out that color. If it strikes granite, it just comes out.

Baptism

Earth's most exquisite picture. I have baptized hundreds of people and felt the wonder of the experience move through them. If by immersion, nothing, absolutely nothing, is more beautiful.

Bath Mat

Bath mats are little dry rugs that children like to stand beside.

Battle

Napoleon is reputed to have said that in every battle there is a fifteen minute period in which the battle is decided.

Is it not also true of life also? There is a time that one must act—and decisively.

Unfortunately, very few act with faith and courage at any part of this critical time.

Practically none makes the major move at the optimum moment.

Remember, it was at the fullness of time that God made His major move.

Beatnik

An antihuman human who claims to be human by acting antihuman. Beatnikism is not dying—only the present form of it.

Beats

Two near dead beatniks were fishing, using a hook with no bait, of course.

They were thoroughly enjoying having seceded from the human race, being rooted in the routine of renouncing reality, when all of a sudden an alligator came out of the water and bit off a leg of one of the blasé baskers in the sun.

"Jerome," he yawned, "An alligator just bit off my leg."

"James, are you quite certain?"

"Quite certain, Jerome."

"Which one was it?"

"I don't know. Man, if you've seen one alligator, you've seen them all."

Bed

The best place to write.
Very poor for sleeping.

Bedtime Stories

A sad sociological story that hit me one evening.
Poor man to boisterous little one: "Sammy, honesty is the best policy; trust the Lord. Beans went up three cents today."
Rich man to blanket clutching, thumb sucker: "Linus, Hartford is the best policy. Trust nobody. Your stock went up ½ point today."

Bill Betts

The greatest friend I ever had. It was Jonathan and David all the way.
At 36, this vivacious, powerful, and handsome minister stood in his pulpit to preach, read Galatians 2:20 "I live by the faith of the Son of God . . ." and fell to the floor, dead.
"Tell my Saviour that I'm coming, too!"

Bible Reading

A very great sin these days. The chief parable concerning this: A school principal saw some boys huddled together. "What are you doing?" he demanded.
"We were telling dirty jokes," was the sheepish answer.

"Oh, that's all right. I thought you were praying."

If you really want to know how to read the Bible, let me recommend that you begin reading at the first verse of Matthew's Gospel. Read until you find a specific commandment from Christ. Put down your Bible, go out into the community and put the teaching into practice. Having done this, begin reading where you stopped until you come to another demand from Christ. Put that into practice.

Keep up this process until you have reached the last verse of Matthew.

When you have completed the first book of the New Testament, either you will be hanging from a cross or you will have changed the world.

Bird

A people watcher.

Blues

Adam had 'm.

Boat

That which keeps the people in and the water out. New religious movement with more Sunday worshippers than any other church. A boat is a hole in the water surrounded by wood into which you pour money.

Books

A method of living with great minds of all ages. Dead authors never feel slighted if you break them off in the middle of a paragraph. A decade later you can resume the discussion on the exact word where you stopped.

Books are dangerous because they present frozen ideas. Once printed, they are as irretrievable as a hiccup. A method of making oneself omnipresent . . . a form of immortality.

I think of my library as a miniature heaven where I am surrounded by the greats of every age. A man's study is a most holy place.

Boy

Dirty noise. A father's image conveyor, a mother's nerve titillater. Steals hearts and cookies . . . odor of a mountain goat . . . an enemy of starch and stillness.

James Bradford

This wonderful friend, now in Heaven, was a warm, earthy, straightforward minister.

He closed a sermon with an illustration about a house afire and the heroism of a man who dashed in and out of the house saving first the mother, then a son, then a daughter, then another son until all were saved.

After the service, he asked a friend why the congregation seemed bewildered during the closing story.

"I do not know, unless it was the fact that you neglected to mention that the house was on fire."

Bread and Circuses

I am a great fan of Mark Twain, not only for his wit but also for his wisdom. There are more than thirty volumes of his works in my library. He wrote something that sounds strangely modern.

"Rome's liberties were not auctioned off in a day, but were bought slowly, gradually, furtively, little by little; first with a little corn and oil for the exceedingly poor and wretched, later with corn and oil for voters who were not quite so poor, later still with corn and oil for pretty much every man that had a vote to sell . . ."

(Reader's Digest, August, 1963.)

Bull

Husband to a cow . . . gouched by gauchos . . . cowed by cowboys.

A child once wrote that a Papal Bull is a cow kept in Rome to provide milk for the Pope's children.

Howard Butt, Jr.

One of the greatest and most creative laymen of all Christian history. If you think this is an overstatement, study it a mite.

C

Capacity

The capacity for great sin and deep prayer are the opposite ends of the same capacity.

Car

A guided missile.

Cathedrals

The world's most expensive embalming process . . . A tomb for a denomination of dead spirits. A massive moral mortuary.

Character

Should develop more rapidly than the gradual decay of the glands. I little trust a man who at 62 says, "Ho, I will now become a man of character."

Chicken

I had a conversation with a chicken as she crossed the road (she stopped half way because she wanted to lay it on the line) and asked her, "Really now, why do you cross the road?"
Her reply disspelled all questions.
"I heard that on the other side they are laying bricks, and this I've got to see."

Child

That which is on, beside, under, off of, always stepping on, perpetual emotion, a precious problem, a perenial bugger, a heart thief, an ear trumpet.
Greatly loved by deaf people and grandparents.

Children

I love children. It is my firm conviction that this country should be run by children—when they are older, of course.

China

I suspect the tyrants sleep fitfully there. I honestly doubt that they could sustain a major war. Wouldn't it be strange if the United States and the Soviet Union ultimately formed an alliance against that eastern colossus? Strange and very foolish.

The Church

A church is a training school in spiritual matters, equipping humans to adapt that spirituality to every phase of living.

The above statement is the ideal. Unfortunately the latter part of the twentieth century, with its soaring scientism and materialism, has a church that is far below the ideal.

There are several reasons for the lagging church. Some of them are here listed (as I see it):

1. *Denominational complexity that eliminates individual creativity.* "You can't suggest that because of article three under section two."

2. *Ministerial jealousy.* "That's a good idea Mac, but it will never work in our church."

3. *The rise of relativism.* "I don't believe you can apply that everywhere. It's really how you look at it."

4. *Biblical vivisection.* "Are you sure criticism will allow that?"

5. *Deemphasized eschatology.* "What, should I preach on the Second Coming when there are so many sociological problems that need our attention?"

6. *Fascination with flairs.* "He is an old fashioned Bible preacher. His method is the finest preaching of the nineteenth century. My people want me to deal with some real issues, issues they are facing."

7. *Fear of power structures in the church.* "You offend Mr. Ipswitch once more and he'll begin a campaign for your removal. He has done it before. You see, he has business connections with practically every leader in the church . . ."

8. *Maximizing the sins of the flesh above those of the spirit.* "That was a real sermon on fleshly lusts. It really applies to old Smith. You know what I heard about him . . ."

9. *Increased emphasis on professional soul winners.* "Pastor, I'll do anything you ask except that. I don't want people to think I'm a hard nose. We really won people when we had that evangelist here last year."

10. *Substitution of deeper life conferences for revivals.* "I really get a little tired of hearing a simple 'Come to Christ' sermon. Let's go a little deeper."

18

11. *Substitution of revivals for deeper life conferences.* "Man, if a person is truly born again, he is equipped to face any problem in life . . ."
12. *Failure to guard the fellowship of the church.* "We can't afford to offend Mrs. Scream. She's hopping mad again and says she has something to bring up at business meeting."
13. *Emphasis upon ethics without reference to Biblical faith.* "Pastor, why preach on the Holy Spirit in human life? We need to forget that and deal with slum clearance."
14. *Emphasis upon niceties of the Biblical faith without references to moral character.* "Now, Mr. Luciano, the pretribulation as opposed to the mid-tribulation. . . . ."
15. *Pride in unknowables.* "Now, I know what you good people of Horse Switch are thinking. You're thinking, 'Pastor, that last statement smacks of Arianism.' "
16. *Lack of respect for leaders.* "Now that he has politicked his way into that position, let's see how well he can do without our cooperation."
17. *Considering zeal a characteristic of the immature Christian.* "Pastor, the new converts can take those visitation assignments. (I hope they get over this door knocking bit; it embarrasses the church.) "
18. *Being unaware of institutional dry rot.* "The Mother Church must set the tone of spiritual serenity in the community."
19. *Statistics becoming the only measuring rod of spiritual success.* "Let's have an evangelistic service for the seven year olds. We must beat our last year's record."

Church

Once courageous—now docile . . . occasionally epileptically enthusiastic—then back to hibernation. Has more power than all governments but is afraid to unleash it. Will never mean much so long as it waits to see which way the wind blows before announcing its "convictions."

19

Church Bells

I become heartsick when I hear of a city which allows a football stadium, race tracks, or a gymnasium filled with screaming fans and will frown upon granting a permit to a church enabling it to install church bells on the ground that it violates an anti-noise ordinance.

Church Buildings

The greatest heresy of them all. When the churches adopted the use of buildings as the only places of worship, God was put in a box and the masses were shut out. All church leaders will admit the difficulty of persuading the common man of the streets to come inside a magnificent edifice.

The only place Jesus failed was inside a building. His greatest sermon is not entitled "The Sermon in the Cathedral" but "The Sermon on the Mount."

The beautifully ornate, architecturally perfect front door of a church may have sent more men to perdition than the liquor industry.

The Temple idea was done away with at the death of Christ. The veil of the Temple was destroyed. God became universally available. Man could meet him anywhere: at the shops, in the fields, in their homes. Then we put Him back into another Temple called "the Church House." Later the name was shortened to "Church."

Now the majority of people think of church as a building—and we are right back where we were before Jesus died. Ask the man on the street where one finds God. He will point to the nearest "church."

If only we can rediscover the wonder that Christ is roaming the earth seeking hearts in which to live: that the person is the Temple of the Holy Spirit; that divine service is rendered at the stove or the sink, in the garage, or at the cash register. If only we can learn this, we shall have begun the new Reformation.

This, Cecil Sherman calls "Wren's Rot." Ross Coggins calls it "The Oedifice Complex."

Church Offerings

The churches are suffering from a bad case of "shell out falter." There is too much month at the end of the money. An offering plate is the outstretched, pleading hand of a missionary doctor badly in need of supplies, war orphans wondering about the next bowl of rice, hospitals, colleges, the education of young ministers and a hundred other most noble and worthy causes. The most spiritual part of a service is the offering, for there we prove our faith with our works.

Church Problems

I read an analysis of the crash of the Hindenberg. This accident was caused by the gas chambers being in too close proximity to each other. This is the greatest known cause of church problems: too many gas bags too close together.

Church Suppers

I hate to see a church try to finance itself by oyster suppers. It makes as much sense as a restaurant asking for contributions.

Church Union

There is a difference between church union and church unity. You can tie a dog's tail and a cat's tail together, then toss them over a clothesline. You may have union but you certainly won't have unity.

Cinderella's Slipper

Young ladies, always try to get your foot in it. Don't you ever believe that fairy tale that says Prince Charming doesn't exist. The denial of his existence was a story written by unrealistic people for unfanciful adults. These people are very ill and need to see a psychiatrist.

Civil Rights

A method devised to make it possible for men to resort to uncivil methods to attain or frustrate equality for all men.

During the Little Rock crisis, a disk jockey in Central Africa said, "People who live in white houses should not throw Little Rocks."

Cocktails

Probably necessary to anesthetize men against the fact that their nation is in the process of decay.

Coeducation

Recently Texas A & M College made two major changes in their program. The institution was completely integrated and girls were allowed to enroll.

There was no complaint about integration, but there has been a tremendous din of noise in protest to the girls attending A & M. In fact, the Aggie Alumni have marched on the capitol in Austin.

Ken Day, obviously pro Texas University or Baylor, told me that some scientists could not understand this behavior. So, to see what makes an Aggie tick, they crossed an Aggie with a gorilla. The result was a retarded gorilla.

Cold

A Mexican hairless dog in a Wyoming snow-storm.

Comedy

Comedy had real purpose-diversion in the old days. No one is as funny as Harold Lloyd, Buster Keaton, Fatty Arbuckle, the Keystone Cops, or Ben Turpin.

These modern comics rely on their ability to stand up and repeat what Jack Douglas wrote for them. I believe that any person of slightly above average talent could become, with practice, a successful modern comic.

I nearly wept for one of those poor souls once. Appearing on the Jack Paar Show, he forgot his lines. I died ten times in pure sympathy. Buster Keaton would not have been at sea if this happened. He would simply have executed one of those exquisitely beautiful pratfalls—and the audience would have been in stitches.

Commercial

Wouldn't the following be an interesting station breaker: "Friends, death is nature's way of telling us to slow down." Huh?

G. P. Comer

There never will be another character like him. He sings Christmas carols in the finest stores of Dallas, leads patriotic songs in public cafeterias and formerly quiet restaurants, and manifests other such evidences of humility.

Hundreds of stories—all true—can be told about this unusual man. Space and nerve limit me to just one of them.

When G. P. Comer was pastor of the First Methodist Church of Waco, Texas, he was conducting a Sunday evening service and called upon a young, enthusiastic minister to lead in prayer. The prayer, with asides by Reverend Comer, went like this:

Minister: "O Lord, Thou hast said in the second chapter of Acts that all of a sudden darkness would come upon the face of the earth as the sun shall be turned to darkness."

Comer: "My Lord, how will we see to get around?"

Minister: "We will call Washington, D. C. and they will say, 'It's dark!' "

Comer: "They've been in the dark for twenty years!"

Minister: "We will call Toronto and it will be dark. We will call London and it will be dark. We will call Paris and it will be dark. We will call Moscow, Berlin, Copenhagen, Stockholm, Calcutta, Rome, Athens and it will be dark!"

Comer: "What a phone bill!"

Committee

A good committee is made up of three people, two of whom are dead. One intelligent person, given all the facts, can do a better job in 60% of the time required by a committee.

Common Sense

That sense without which sense all other sense is nonsense.

Communism

A philosophy that everybody will share what little the land can produce under such a sorry system. If Communism could produce the dynamic individuals that come from the free enterprise system, it might be able to rise to mediocrity. But it can't do it. Therefore, it will die due to its inability to fulfill its promises.

Any system that must resort to terror to remain in power will ultimately die.

It is tragic that Russia and China must go through this rigorous and extravagant education before discovering the free enterprise system.

Instead of losing millions of lives, all they must do is take an objective look at the United States and observe its happy people who have such a wonderful system that the poor people eat better than the favored of most other nations.

Compassion . . .

. . . is not a snob gone slumming. Anybody can salve his conscience by an occasional foray into knitting for the spastic home.

Did you ever take a *real* trip down inside the broken heart of a friend? To feel the sob of the soul—the raw, red crucible of emotional agony? To have this become almost as much yours as that of your soul crushed neighbor?

Then, to sit down with him—and silently weep? This is the beginning of compassion.

Computers

A new book has been released for computers entitled, "How To Understand People."

I heard two computers talking one day. "What is the greatest threat facing machine-kind today?" one of them asked.

"Peoplization" was the reply.

Conversation

A habit that characterized the decadent days of man before television . . . a lost art.

Conversion

A converted man has the same old bulge in his pocket. It is made by a Bible instead of a flask.

Calvin Coolidge

Calvin Coolidge used to say there were four important maxims:

"Eat it up
Wear it out
Make it do
Do without."

Coolidge wasn't the only one to say that. I've heard these statements from church finance committees for the last twenty years. I do wish they would find a new president.

Cooperative Apartments

Cordwood of cramped creatures who seem to enjoy it.

Sam Coots

One of those great characters who crosses your trail leaving you better because of it is Sam Coots, a Christian gentleman from Owensboro, Kentucky.

He is full of great stories that could fill a dozen books.

When I was his pastor, Mr. Coots told me the same stories again and again at my request.

One of those Coots' yarns went like this: Over a hundred years ago, Reuben Cottrell was the pastor of the First Baptist Church of Owensboro. The first Republican Convention ever held in Kentucky met in that city. The moderator of the meeting noticed Reverend Cottrell, a staunch Democrat, seated in the crowd and asked Brother Reuben to pronounce the invocation for the Republican convention.

Cottrell sank down in his chair and whispered, "Excuse me, I don't want the Lord to know I'm here!"

Mr. Coots told of a Kentucky mountain philosopher who agreed to "say the words" at the funeral of a village tough, which service none of the pastors cared to conduct. His words at the graveside were brief enough:

"He wasn't as bad all the time as he was most of the time."

That reminds me of the colored pastor who accepted the responsibility for preaching the funeral of a rather notorious character. When asked if he would tell the people that the deceased would go to Heaven or Hell, he replied: "Neither, I'll just funeralize him right up to the banks of the river, then let whoever he belongs to come and get him."

Counseling

Some pastors have gone so far in pastoral counseling that if one of them saw a young man drowning, he would lean over the bank and say, "Son, would you like to tell me about it?" or "When did you first sense that you were beginning to drown?"

Courage

Not every church that says it wants its minister to be a man of courage would put up with him if he became one.

How long has it been since you stood with a minority for a principle you love?

Courage

Some chicken friends of mine were playing a game. They all lined up by the side of the road, and at the last minute, jumped at swift moving cars passing by. If one of them lost his nerve at the last minute, the other chickens would sneeringly say to him, "Teenager!"

Cow

The holy animal for the peace of mind cult . . . victim of automation . . . when milked, she's proud but pooped.

Coward

One of those neutral nobodies who is a perfectly blended part of the landscape . . . a vacuumed soul . . . the cube root of nothing . . . a pathetic actor in the theatre of compromise.

He dies in the valley of indecision during the battle between guilt and conformity.

Del Crandell

The famous catcher for the Milwaukee Braves spoke in our church one Sunday evening. I asked him if Christ made a difference on the playing field. His answer was shockingly wonderful.

"No, I can't say that there is a great deal of difference between a Christian and a non-Christian ball player. But that isn't the end of the story. Every father dreams of having a son who is a fine athlete. This has been especially true with me. The Lord has blessed our home with five children. The two boys are mentally retarded. My friends, this is where Christ makes all the difference in the world."

Creativity

If we will put all our eggheads in one basket, something will hatch.

Creativity comes like the crumbling of a dike: first a trickle, then a stream, finally a deluge. It is born in quietude and contemplation.

We sometimes think great creativity is born in the midst of titanic effort. Actually, it might be a good idea for the nation to declare a moratorium on work for two weeks, send our scientists to Glorieta, New Mexico or Ridgecrest, North Carolina to listen to the silence, pray to the Creator, and let their subconscious juices begin to flow.

Critic

Did you ever see a statue erected to a critic? Take the stones critics throw at you and build a super market. Sell the supermarket and live off the interest of the profit made. Buy a Cadillac and give your critics a free ride.

Take the stones the critics throw at you and build a factory. Someone has to provide employment for the critics. Some critics do their work in the name of Christianity. God wants spiritual fruit, not religious nuts.

Criticism

A method conceived by the atalented to cause them to feel equal to the multitalented . . . most often a child of jealousy.

Cursing

Verbal sewage. To learn to quit: start substituting your mother's name for God's. This is proof that we love mother but not God.

D

Daughter

A heart thief . . . giggles in ribbons . . . a daddy melter.
A perfect person who marries the village idiot.

Deafness

When introducing two people, whisper to each that the other is
very hard of hearing. Then watch them scream at each other.

Death

I have witnessed scores of deaths. From an objective, coldly
scientific view, I can report that at the moment of death, an exit is
made. *Something* leaves the body, changing it from an animated
organism to a valueless protoplasm.

Jesus, who went through the experience, said that we should
not be disturbed. In His Father's home there is plenty of room.
That is where the soul takes its journey.

Birth is the beginning of death; death is the birth of life—eternal life.

To the man in Christ there should never be fear.

Dedication

The ability to continue in a resolution after the emotion in which the resolution was made has vanished.

Democrat

A modern Democrat is one who has discovered a vote getting system based on the repudiation of original Democratic principles.

Dentist

He gets on my nerves.

Deprojectmanagerization

When an army project is well enough along to move on without a manager, the armed forces deprojectmanagerize it.

This is the very thing a pastor should do. Any church project should be so well organized, the personnel so well trained, the purposes so well defined that the pastor can let it run by itself. An occasional refueling of prayer and encouragement from the pastor should be all that is needed.

I would change the military term to "deprojectpastorizing."

Desk

If a cluttered desk means a cluttered mind, what does an empty desk mean?

Despondency

When a tired body and a negative mind meet.

Devil

Some people deny his existence—I don't. I've done business with him too long to do that.

A Christianity diluted into a happy and sensible religion, in which God's redemptive act in Christ has dropped out of centrality, is Satan's religion.

The idea that Satan is a red man with horns and a pitchfork is also one of his masterpieces.

He is the top hidden persuader—the master of subliminal motivation.

Diary

When I was very young I kept a day by day account of my activities. I wrote it thinking how interesting it would be when I became internationally famous.

A few years ago, I found it in an old trunk. No sooner had I begun reading it than I fell into a deep sleep. When I wakened, I immediately destroyed it.

Anything *that* boring deserves to die.

Dictionary

It never contains the words for which I am searching.

Diet

The finest food to cause one to lose weight in a hurry is doughnut holes. I have eaten as many as 362 of them in a day and never gained an ounce.

A teenager admired my tie, calling it a "rainbow tie." When I asked him why he called it that, he replied, "Because there is the pot at the end of it."

Another wonderful young hot blood touched my tummy and called it "pirate's treasure." Explained: "sunken chest."

I believe the Darwinian theory: "survival of the fattest."

Discipline

Having heard an elderly pastor preach, a young minister said, "I would give everything I own to be able to preach like that."

"That is exactly what it cost me," the old man replied.

Discipline and Disciple are brother words.

Divorce

One of our greatest problems is not only the hasty marriage but also the hasty divorce.

As a minister I have seen scores of couples who, because of hot headedness and pride, have proceeded with divorce action.

35

A few months pass by and the two stand, looking longingly across the miles, wishing before God they hadn't done it. The same hotheadedness and pride keep them from the road back.

"I've remarried several couples. It isn't the worst idea in the world.

Someone asked if Doris and I had ever thought of divorce. The answer is that we have not thought of divorce but we have considered murder on a few occasions.

Divorce

Nearly 51% of the divorces of the world take place in the United States, 6% of the world's population.

The ministers who try to help deserve assistance and encouragement—not censure.

Tandem polygamy.

Single file harems.

Doorknobs

The world's greatest field of Christian service is opened by them. I love a minister whose heart is in his shoes as he walks the witness in a wilderness of watchers.

Downtown Church

Most denominations think a city is like a doughnut: active churches in the suburbs, where the dough is, and a gaping hole where there is no dough.

Drinking

Most imbibers arrive at a solution when they read so much about the bad effects of drinking alcohol.

With firm resolve, they give up reading.

E

E.S.P.

I really believe in it if it stands for Extra Sincere People.

East Germany

The East German government has released an eight volume socialist encyclopedia.

One major and significant omission: the word "love."

Jake Edmunds

My next door neighbor at Glorieta, J. P. Edmunds, is formerly the statistician of the Southern Baptist Convention.

He loves to quote Benjamin Franklin: "One of the tragedies of life is the murder of a beautiful theory by a gang of brutal facts."

Effervescence

I am writing this while basking in the morning sun, seated in my reclining chair on the porch of *El Ranchito Chiquito* on my "spread" in New Mexico (five miles by sixty five feet—perfect for raising very slender cattle.)

The background noises are better than Muzak. My son practicing on his new guitar (it will be a while before he is another Segovia) ; the clear voice of my girl child singing a song she learned at lakeside services in the valley: "Red and yellow, black and white, they are precious in His sight! Jesus loves the little children of the world"; my neighbors, the Jake Edmunds—finest people on earth, chatting with a visitor about the common topic of these hills; nothing—a great, good sound; my buddy, Topper, a diminutive little jerk of a bird with leather lungs, destroying the decibels (Seismograph crew in L. A., please note.) from atop a tall pine (I wish he'd move his church letter to the Presbyterian encampment.)

At any rate, it's one of those "God's in His heaven, all's right with the world" mornings. I feel I have discovered a cure for which there is no sickness, called health.

It isn't great preaching services that make me hit the sawdust trail. Sheer undiluted gratitude to the good Lord for giving me and mine a sound body, a composed spirit, an inner joy, and an opportunity to serve and feel purposefully used drives me to my knees faster than anything.

Eggs

Like people, get hard boiled when in hot water.

Ego

From me to me with lots of love . . .

Ego

There are two kinds of egotists: those who admit it, and the rest of us.

Egotist

He is the devil incarnate. He thinks if he had not been born, God would feel the loss and the world would wonder why . . .

An "I" specialist who would want his epitaph to read "Run to the hills; abandon hope; George Sludgewater is dead."

Energy

The early bird arose very early to get the worm but discovered that the worm was gone.

Some other bird had worked all night.

Engagement

On the verge with an urge to merge; when a young couple lean on each other like a sick kitten against a warm brick.

Before marriage, when she trips on a stone, he says, "What's the matter, snookums, did oo stump your itsey-bitsey toe?"

After marriage: "Whatsa' matter, you big ox, can't you walk?"

People on the brink of committing matrimony.

England

A great, old nation that has manifested unusual greatness in yielding up its colonial system. This is one of the most noble acts of modern times. Badly in need of Serutan.

Epitaph

Said of a man who cannot talk back . . . belated flattery . . . kind words which if said earlier might have caused him to be alive today.

Escapism

Someone preached a great sermon entitled "Nailing up the Back Door." I don't recall the details of the message, but wouldn't it make an excellent sermon about the present, prevalent philosophy of escapism?

You aren't happy where you are? You know you will be perfectly suited for New York or Dallas—is that it?

You are sure the present wife is not for you—another somebody would be much more to your liking? You need to nail up the back door.

Don't be like the converted gambler who kept a deck of cards "just in case I backslide."

I won't soon forget a wonderful Christian mother, Martiele Akers, whose son, Michael, had lost his life in a plane crash, giving advice to a mother who had just suffered the same agonizing loss: "Don't take tranquilizers, my dear; you must go *through* it, not *around* it."

No back door for her.

Go through sorrow, responsibility, or guilt—you'll come out more of a person, more Christ's man or woman.

Evangelist

In spite of Sinclair Lewis' autobiography, *Elmer Gantry,* the story of what Lewis would have been if he had been an evangelist, I still believe that great spiritual and social good is accomplished by these dedicated men.

Few people realize the sacrifice of time, finances, and family made by them. I know the mass image producers have pictured the evangelist as a sartorial monstrosity who dresses like a sad sax player who delivers a twisted mouthed carnival barker type canned talk; an Elvis Presley sans guitar who deals with the double shuffle and the long green.

I challenge these journalists to find one—just one—such person in the major Protestant denominations. If they can't do it, for the sake of the image of God's men, they ought to shut up.

"Angels are still bright, though the brightest fell."—Shakespeare.

Evasion

The churches have two choices before them: deal with pertinent issues or die.

Blessed are the people who fearlessly and intelligently deal with the sociological issues surging in the world.

Some churches have learned to read the times so well that they can run away well in advance of the explosive social earthquakes.

But a generation or two of such running and they die of fear and exhaustion.

Evening Worship Service

Dr. C. Grier Davis at Montreat, North Carolina, quoted an Episcopalian rector friend of his as saying he was sure Nicodemus could not have been an Episcopalian because no Episcopalian would have sought Jesus at night.

Dorcas Everly

I told her as she was dying. "Remember, to our Father a day is as a thousand years. If that is true, an hour is as forty years and forty years is as an hour. You will soon be leaving your husband and two girls. He will be away from you an hour at the most; the two girls not more than two hours. You will think they have been at grandmother's farm for a brief visit."

We are not at the mercy of the grim impartiality of the caprice of the toss of fate's dice.

Evil

Evil can run a mile while the church is putting on its shoes.

Exaggeration

When Stalin died, Pravda reported that a certain number of people marched by his casket per hour. The report said they came four abreast.

An Oklahoma State University Math Professor stated the Russian boast that they are the greatest athletes in the world must be true since in order to accomplish what Pravda said they did, the people had to run by Stalin's bier faster than Bob Hayes's world record 9.1 for the one hundred yard dash.

Exercise

That which will cause your body to last a lifetime.

F

FDR

The nicest bad man and the worst good man of the twentieth century.

FAD

The latest fad is City Blaming.

The whole city of Dallas, including its public schools, beautiful churches, Southern Methodist University, Baylor Hospital, its businesses, its children, its old people—all of them have received the blame for the assassination of President Kennedy.

This indicates the profound wisdom of the advocates of this new fad.

By the same reasoning New York City and New Orleans are partially guilty of pulling the trigger because Lee Harvey Oswald once passed *through* those cities. Los Angeles is guilty because he wrote a letter to that city at one time. Pittsburg is guilty because he mentioned it in conversation. Philadelphia is very greatly to be blamed because Oswald *must have thought of it at one time or another.*

Birmingham is an ideal city for this new fad. One of the largest newspapers in Chicago had a real field day with Birmingham for weeks after the terrible bombing of the Sixteenth Street Baptist Church, which no Birminghamian in his right mind attempted to justify.

The Chicago journalists *should* have condemned the act which occurred in Birmingham but it is very incorrect it was done *by* Birmingham.

The pious pressmen in the Windy City overlooked the fact that there were seventy-two bombings in Chicago in one year—all unsolved.

It would be very inappropriate to blame the great city of Chicago or the excellent police force of that city for these terrible deeds or the fact that they were unsolved. The most difficult sort of crime to solve is a bombing.

New York City does not deserve the blame for the Harlem race riots. I doubt that 99 per cent of Harlem had anything to do with it.

For the southern press to cheer when the problems of racial tension flared up in the north struck me as an evidence of just how popular City Blaming has become.

I realize how unpopular my view may be to those who delight in public panning but really it is time to pan the public panners.

Let's face it.

One man in Dallas shot John F. Kennedy—the remaining 750 thousand residents of that really fine city had absolutely nothing to do with his death.

Perhaps only a few were responsible for the church bombing in Birmingham, the remaining 600,000 are not guilty of that specific act.

I would bet a red button that not more than fifty Negroes were directly responsible for the Harlem riots. One cannot lay the blame on the Negro community for the act.

This is not to condone the spreading of venom by hate groups both liberal and conservative or cultivating the climate of suspicion.

But it is downright fascistic (here's a switch) for certain extremist liberal groups to make *all* of Dallas or Birmingham guilty by association. It is pure hypocrisy for southerners to blame *every* New York Negro for Harlem.

Let us attack this game of tossing guilt from one section of the country to another, thus creating national hatreds, fraternal feuds, and community finger pointing.

Our country has never been more in need of Christian love and understanding.

America could be changed if all sections of the nation would heed but one chapter from the Bible, First Corinthians, chapter 13.

They said of the early Christians, "Behold how they love one another!"

They say of modern ones, "Behold how they club one another."

Failure

A great task lay before him, so he increased the latent potential of his laziness and ended up a beautiful failure.

It is impossible to grow tired doing the things you most enjoy. Men rarely fail doing that which gives them the most pleasure.

But if you fail and have the proper attitude toward it, you are a success. Often, failure is the greatest success. I have seen successes that were really failures.

Remember, neither success nor failure is permanent. If you are in the bleakness of failure, be aware that only at night have new worlds been discovered.

Never try to please everyone; never try to displease everyone. Between these two poles is your success.

Operate on the basis of conviction rather than accommodation; but accommodate everyone up to the point of your convictions.

It is always right to do right. It is always wrong to do wrong. It is never right to do wrong. It is never wrong to do right.

Success is the line of most resistance to the forces working for failure. Discover what those forces are and fight like heaven against them

Be lazy; there's always room at the bottom. Think on the epitaph of a famous mountain guide: "He died climbing."

Fallibility

We are constantly being assured that there is no danger of an accidental releasing of nuclear energy. Yet Charles Wells, the eminent Christian journalist, claims that a bomber accidentally dropped an H-Bomb over North Carolina. There are six triggers that must be released in order to detonate the bomb and five of the triggers had been tripped.

If trigger six had also been released, there would now be no North Carolina.

Additionally, how would we have convinced ourselves that this was not an attack from the Soviet Union?

We would then have attacked Russia, demolishing her. She would have countered and the United States would be no more.

We have already been one trigger release away from eternity. When will we learn the absolute fallibility of our present course?

I am convinced we will never be taught the proper way so long as our economy is geared to national defense.

I remember Dr. M. L. Fergeson of Baylor University stating that if we made it impossible to profit from war production, there could be no war.

I disagreed with my old professor then. But he was so right.

Fanatic

If you express emotion when Hank Aaron hits a round tripper—you are a fan. If you express emotion concerning your faith—you are a fanatic.

My Favorite Food

I can eat and enjoy anything but celery and razor blades.
I am almost certain that I would like okra if I ever had a chance

to taste it. I don't know what's gotten into okra. It just doesn't trust itself. When it is picked up by the fork and is making its way to the mouth, its inferiority feelings begin to manifest themselves. I am almost certain I heard an okra from Oklahoma say to itself one time, "Will he *really* like me? I'll be all right if I'm *sure* he likes me. But why *should* he like me? Why should *anybody* like me? What have I to offer that would *make* him like me? I know, I can feel it way down deep inside—he *won't* like me. I wish I were dead. Well, if that's the kind he is—the sort of person who goes around not liking okra . . . I'll show him. He'll never know about *me* . . . zzzzzip."

The okra was gone.

If only he had given me a chance to like him. I believe I could have really enjoyed him but he just wouldn't trust himself. There's something wrong with the whole race of okras.

Mass hysteria, mass insecurity, I call it. Do you know a psychiatrist who specializes in okra? They need help. If only someone would have nerve enough to just up and tell them, someone with real compassion.

My Favorite Game

Sitting in my vibrator chair, watching the room get all shook up. It is time the room got shook up. It has been steady as Gibraltar for years. Always *I'm* nervous, trembling like a leaf in a blizzard. For once, matter trembles and only I am stable, secure, unmoveable. Tremble, old room, tremble!

Fearlessness

One of the most outstanding displays of depth courage I ever witnessed was seeing about 500 grown men and women booing a frail little six year old Negro child as she slowly walked into a previously all white school.

These adults were reflecting the sort of courage Americans have never revealed before.

Courage like this was not in evidence at the Argonne Forest, Iwo Jima, and Heartbreak Ridge.

This is the new courage.

Florida

There are two places you will really enjoy in Florida: on the beach and off it.

The only place I have ever been where I want to go where I have just been so I can see it again.

My adopted state—my, how I wish I had been born there. I think only 9 people over twenty years of age are natives.

Food

Having eaten at some of the most heavily ladened festive boards as well as at the tables of some Old Mother Hubbards (of bare cupboard fame) it would be possible for me to write an excellent little book entitled *Gospel Gastronomy*.

I was born with an appetite as ravenous as a Dempster Dumpster and taste buds that responded positively to everything with the possible exception of Grasshoppers.

Many times there have been groanings that could not be uttered by this overloaded sinner. My belt became a leather fence around a chicken graveyard. I have been responsible for helping many sons of the fabled rooster to enter the ministry.

Foreign Aid

We think we can cure the world's ills by rubbing gold into them.

Foreign Aid

Money we give to the nations that seem to need it. This enables them to attain such a position of status that they can afford to ignore us.

Wendel and Edith Foster

Their first child was a spastic. They asked Jesus to give them love for this little helpless daughter.

The Lord did such a good job of it that Wendel and Edith started taking in other spastic children.

Today they care for more than sixty of these precious kids—and have a waiting list of 500 or more.

You must not ask the Lord to give you His love to share if you don't want Him to do it.

Fox Hunters

The most imaginative exaggeraters in the world. Fishermen are a poor second and crowd estimators are a close third.

B. B. Crimm was the best and the worst fox hunter I ever knew. He was an eccentric, yet greatly used, evangelist of a generation ago.

Once I asked him how many people heard him preach the night before.

"About three and a half acres of 'em" he blandly replied.

Crimm preached throughout the southwest in his own tent. Behind the tent were the pens that housed his hunting dogs who accompanied him to every meeting. They were a part of his evangelistic team. He preached while sitting in a cane bottom chair to, as he said, acres of people.

Sometimes his hounds would fight and yelp, interrupting the service.

Crimm, half loving it, would scream, "Dadgummit, you kids shut up! I'm trying to preach the Gospel . . . now, be quiet!"

The "kids" would become as silent as before morning stillness.

Cowboy Crimm hunted sinners all day and foxes all night . . .

. . . and caught many of them.

His recipe for fox hunters' coffee was wonderful enough to warm the cockles of a ditch digger's heart. "It's simple," he said, "You put a bucket on an open fire, a horse shoe in the bottom of the bucket, coffee grounds on top of the horseshoe, fill it up with Louisiana swamp water. Then you boil it.

"When the horseshoe comes to the top, it's ready."

Man, that's coffee.

France

Happy duplicity . . . beautiful flowers, beautiful girls, beautiful saps. Never look a Frenchman in the eye—always watch his hands.

A Friend . . .

. . . in need will worry you to death.

Frustration

Superannuated beauty queens, old authors, ministers in a society given over to idolatry.

Furniture

Some furniture goes back to Louis the fourteenth; ours goes back to Sears the fifteenth.

G

Zsa Zsa Gabor

Publicly a sex symbol; privately dead on her feet—a really interesting conversationalist and a more altruistic person than one would imagine.

Doris and I do not know her well enough to call her by her first Zsa but well enough to appreciate her.

Garden

If you really want peace of mind, call someone to come do your gardening while you go to the theatre.

Gentleman

Is always kind to dogs and cats.
He is also sometimes nice to people.

Barry Goldwater

A pretty great profile in courage—if you'll excuse the expression.

Golf

If a minister shoots a high score, he is neglecting his golf; if he shoots a low one, he is neglecting his church.

Actually I don't know which end of the caddy to hold.

Gossip

The town crier . . . peddler of pious piffler, meanest person in town . . . only sin meriting capital punishment, should be hanged by the tongue . . . a limber lip. There is no more contemptuous person . . . makes hell seem justifiable.

Billy Graham

Thoroughly sincere Christian in spite of all the image makers have done to make us suspect otherwise. I know him. He's solid as granite.

Greed

Man's nature demands acquisitiveness. It has been said of LBJ that all he wants is all there is.

A Mrs. Lurana Fidelia Stribling, who built a fantastic land empire around Johnson City, Texas, was asked how much she aspired to possess. She answered, "I don't want it all. All I want is all my own and all that joins it."

Grits

Georgia ice cream. Never trust a man who doesn't like grits and put very little confidence in those who do.

Clu Gulagher

I went to Baylor when Clu was a student there. We always knew he would end up but the question was—where? He made a step in the right direction when he married Miriam Nethery. She was a beautiful and thoroughly dedicated coed, who sang with us in youth meetings. Clu landed the role of Billy the Kid in the TV series "The Tall Man" and his fame was assured.

Once Clu and Miriam visited her home church, the First Baptist Church of Pine Bluff, Arkansas. The service came to an end, and the pastor, Dr. Robert Smith, called on Clu to pronounce the benediction.

This was totally unexpected, and Clu was not exactly internationally known as the year's outstanding public supplicator. In fact, he had never done it before in his whole life.

The cowboy was not to be outdone, so he sauntered to the pulpit and prayed a prayer that the church won't soon forget.

"Lord, help us to get behind whatever it is the preacher is pushing. Lord, I sure do like this church. As you know, I have a little red-headed boy and I would give just anything if he could grow up in a church like this. There aren't any churches like this out in California. In fact, Lord, you ain't got much going out there. I hope you will soon. Amen."

H

John Haggai

A minister friend whom I greatly admire. I kid him by telling him that I was praying for him and the Lord replied, "John Haggai? Where is he now? I haven't heard from him since 1947."

Hairdos

Hairdon'ts or hairshouldn'ts. May God forgive the hairdressers.

Hankerin'

An actual letter—as received—in the office of the First Baptist Church of West Palm Beach, Florida.

Ft. Piers, Fla.

Sep—17—1962

Deare Brother Baptest

I seen on the telvishion over the Brodecastion Stashion that there was 1 or 2 widows down there maby more that wanted a good husben I am a widow By death I am a Beaptest here yn Ft Pierse ef you can give me some names an adresses y will be very glad one or more y am unterested please let me heare soon and yours truly,

m. g.

hill haven—Ft.

Pierse Fla

Hands

There are hands that disturb me.
The downstretched hands from heaven,
The upstretched hands from hell,
The outstretched hands of broken humanity,
The folded hands of the church, and
The pleading hands of Jesus Christ.
These hands keep me awake at night.

Harmony

The nations of the earth could make this tight little planet a nice place to live if they would learn the power of international harmony. I do wish Mr. Kosygin, Mao Tse Tung, and Charles DeGaulle would take music lessons.

Hat

Once my hat was used to receive the offering when someone had mislaid the offering plates. My exfriend, Bob Randall, remarked that this was the first time that the hat had any "cents" in it.

Ray Rozell weighed 130 pounds dripping wet. He looked like an elongated breadstick. When offered a giant Texas hat as a gift, he declined with his Texas drawl: "Naw, I don't want it. If I wore that thing I would look like a dadgum thumb tack!"

. . . a warmer for nude knobs.

Haywool County, N. C.

It was Haywool County Day at Lake Junaluska. Dr. Carlyle Marney was scheduled to preach for the occasion.

"What shall I use as a text for my sermon?" Dr. Marney asked an old timer.

The old Mountain William pondered a moment, then said, "I wish you would use my favorite verse, which reads, "If you can't buy it in Haywool County, you don't need it!"

Heaven

Happy, debonair, humorous Christians cause people to want to go to heaven. Many people think they prefer hell to living forever with some of the sour religious samples who bore the daylights out of you. Be assured of one thing: Jesus couldn't stand their super holy attitude either. He hammered at them broadside with great unsubtlety.

The painfully religious are the cause of more doubt than all the Bertrand Russells combined.

Having been in the ministry several years and met thousands of the good Lord's children, I can assure anyone that He has hosts of children who are humble, happy and hilarious.

They make the urbane, sick, bored secularists seem, at their best, an indigestion brown.

A rock ribbed follower of the happy Christ has more fun at a funeral than a non-Christian has at a ball.

I have given both sides a real fling and the non-Christian way tastes very much like swamp water.

Hell

I don't believe I can ever forget an old minister who with solemnity and love, told a rather spoiled, pampered mother, "My dear, you have bought your son a ticket to hell. Now you want *me* to pray that the train *will be* wrecked."

Wouldn't you rather go to heaven by yourself than to hell with everybody patting you *on the back?*

Sour, dour so-called Christians caused Mark Twain to comment, "It's Heaven for climate and Hell for company."

I heard Ralph Langley preach a really great sermon, filled with compassion and love, about hell. In it he told of reading a sign in a restaurant which read "Just because you don't believe in hell is no sign you aren't going there." Ralph also said, "You may not believe in hell now, but I'm sure you will five minutes *after* you get there."

If there were more hell in the pulpit, there would be less in the community.

I believe I have read most of the arguments against hell. Some of them are very cogent and telling. It has been a serious study for me for at least the last fifteen years and I resist it as most humans of sensitivity seem to do. I am not a pious pyrotechnician.

But the one thing that haunts me is the fact that Jesus believed in hell, taught it as a reality, and referred to it ten times as often as he did heaven. The most searching biblical criticism cannot cause Jesus to have taught anything else.

The decision I have had to make is whether to believe Jesus Christ or those who know much less about it than He.

Hellions

Jesus hobnobbed with them. The church would do well to do the same.

I have a friend who tried this once and discovered a glory.

Other church softball teams set the rule: no boy who smokes can play.

My friend set the rule: Only boys who *do* smoke can play. The applicants lined up for two blocks—just the kids he wanted to reach for God. They have yet to lose a game.

Heroes

The difference between being a leader a generation ago and being one now is that *then* leaders were respected. Today, only the most thick skinned dare take the reins.

Heroes are smeared, not reared.

This is a very sad evidence of decay. No nation can remain virile that habitually villifies its heroes.

A very interesting psychological study would be the national need of heroes. Perhaps one of the thermometers of a nation's spiritual temperature is how it handles them.

P. B. Hill

The world must never be allowed to forget this multifaceted jewel of a human being. He was the pastor of what was then among the largest Presbyterian churches in the world; Poet Laureate of Texas; chaplain of the Texas Rangers; father of the World War II air ace, Tex Hill; former missionary to Korea; recipient of more honorary degrees than he could remember; personal friend of scores of world leaders such as William Jennings Bryan, Will Rogers, and Franklin Delano Roosevelt. Dr. Hill was the founder of the Hill Country Cowboy Camp Meeting, where I was privileged to preach for many years.

It was while serving in this capacity that I grew to know Dr. Hill as a father in God, a towering intellect, and an unusually humorous human being.

He loved to relate experiences by the hour and I always had the hours to spare if I knew I could drink in from this unending fountain of human understanding.

Perhaps his best known humorous experience took place many years ago in Virginia.

He had a little friend with an IQ just above that of rocks who shadowed Dr. Hill and almost worshipped him. His little demented friend attended every public and most private functions, always sitting very near the front of the church on all occasions.

Once Dr. Hill was performing the marriage ceremony of two extremely young people, so poor that church mice could have endowed them. The young groom made his existence by pedaling his bicycle, his prize and only possession, about town running errands for the businessmen. The bride was a sweet, naive, happily ignorant little mountain flower.

It was not a wedding attended by the society editor of the town newspaper. But it was attended by Dr. Hill's little shadow with the blind mind.

As the ceremony proceeded the time came for the repeating of the vows. When the groom solemnly avowed ". . . and all my worldly goods I thee endow . . ." the shadow couldn't stand to see such a loss. Slapping his knee dejectedly and wistfully gazing out the window, he sighed loudly, "Well, there goes his bicycle!"

The last sermon I heard Dr. Hill preach was on the subject "Heaven." There he stood wearing his Texas Ranger uniform, surrounded by the sheep and cattle ranchers to whom he had preached many times. The old tabernacle used for the cowboy camp meeting echoed as his strong clear voice proclaimed his dynamic living faith. "In my text Jesus says 'I go to prepare a place for you.' I heard a minister say that Jesus was speaking symbolically when he said this. The Lord did not mean what he said when He said Heaven was a place, this so-called minister claimed.

"Now if that wolf in sheep's clothing is correct, I have wasted 60 years of my time preaching the Gospel. It will not be long before I will cross the chilly river and be in the presence of Jesus Himself. If there is anything that will make a hell out of heaven it will be for me to discover that instead of having gone to a place, I have arrived at a symbol.

"When I die I don't want to go to a symbol, I want to go to a place."

A few weeks later the old warrior went to Heaven. He now knows that it isn't a symbol.

Hiroshima

The low water mark of American morality.

Hole-In-One

I play golf for exercise. You don't get much exercise if you go around making holes-in-one all the time. That's the reason I don't do it.

Holy

The opposite of me.

According to the Puritans, the absence of personality. According to Christ, the presence of it. The cause of wisdom and happiness.

Home

A place to rest in order to store up rambunctiousness for future hellishness . . . the source of a lot of bills . . . hell for mismates; heaven for the likeminded . . . the chief educational institution in the world . . . the University of Understanding.

Home Town

A little old lady from Littlefield, Texas, my old home town, visited our beautiful Chapel-By-The-Lake, with its fountains, reflection pool, pulpit prow and magnificent view of Lake Worth in West Palm Beach, Florida.

I remembered her from the old days, wearing an old fashioned bonnet. Her clear eyes shone with a glow from her leathern face as I introduced her to two of the key men from our church.

After viewing the beauty of the church setting, she spoke toothlessly, "It's awful hard to believe that little old J. C. Moody would ever be the preacher in a place like this. In fact, it's hard t'believe that he is a preacher at all. We always thought he'd end up in the penitentiary!"

This is in front of my church leaders. Such is intelligence which I rate just below plant life.

Honeymoon

The only time both of them will have a new pair of shoes at the same time.

Hootenanny

Jack Linkletter is mistaken. Actually a hootenanny is the hybrid between an owl and a goat.

Horse

An animal whose favorite pastime is people carrying . . they like to go peopleing around . . . I know several of them personally and they are real nice horses when you get to know them . . . boy charmers.

Hotel

I always get a room next to an acne-faced young man who works until midnight. His room contains his clothes and a few odds and ends, including a book entitled *Bugle for Beginners* with horn to match.

Huntley and Brinkley

Like a duet combining Enrico Caruso and Elvis Presley. You decide which is which.

Husband

To keep him, let him go; to lose him, try to keep him.

Hypocrisy

During World War II the erection of a church building was stopped due to the steel shortage. A committee was sent to Washington to persuade the officials in charge that the steel should be allocated for the church. "Can't you, sort of, go around the regulations to get this steel for our church?" one committeeman pressed.

The steel official glowered, "You mean you want us to break the law in order to build a church so your preacher can preach against the corruption in Washington?"

I

A cult of one.

Ignorance

A malady due to a charley horse between the ears.

Illness

I met a pastor who told me he was resigning due to illness—his people were sick of him.

One layman said, "There are two schools of thought about our pastor. People either dislike him or hate him."

Imagination

The greatest nation on earth. No man is born without a lot of it. It can be learned and greatly stimulated. Sanctified imagination sprinkled with grace, grit and greenbacks equals success.

Impatience

Impatience with God's doings is not the mark of the spiritual mind.

Injury

Always keep a pail of water handy. If someone injures you, immediately write the details in the water. Then you will always have a record of it.

Introduction

A very temporary pumping up of the expectations of an audience.

When given a terrible introduction one time, I replied that at long last I have discovered my nationality. I am a Philistine because I have just been slain by the jawbone of an ass.

A very nervous young speaker once answered a grandiose introduction: "I don't appreciate it but I deserve it from the bottom of my heart."

I resent these accusations of character yet I couldn't speak without them.

Invest

If men were as cynical about God as I am about investments, there would be no churches. I have been offered much help with my investments; when I accepted it I was never given any.

J

Japan

I am sure there are little posters, stickers, and plaques all over Japan with a motto inscribed thereon. An interpreter will gladly read it for you. The nearest translation in English is "Forget Pearl Harbor."

Jew

My Lord was a Jew. I would be nothing without Him. My Bible was given to me by the Jews.

I cannot truthfully say I have been mistreated one time by a Jew.

With all this in their favor why should I hate them?

When my son was ten, he reacted to this by saying, "The Jews didn't give us the Bible, the Gideons did!"

Job

I was deeply moved as I heard Charles Culpepper, former missionary to China, pray that God would restore the Chinese Christians as he did Job after the cankerworm had done its damage.

C. Oscar Johnson

After 3.2 beer was allowed on the market, Dr. Johnson told FDR, "Mr. President, I want to tell you that the millions of Baptists in the United States are behind you 96.8%."

Dr. Johnson must weigh nearly three hundred pounds. He loves to tell about lying in the emergency room of a St. Louis hospital. One of his feet was uncovered. An intense young intern entered the room, placed the stethoscope to the bottom of Dr. Johnson's foot, then grimly turned to the nurse and spoke through tightened lips, "The baby is dead."

Keeping up with the Joneses

I learned better when the Joneses declared bankruptcy.

Kindness

Will open more doors than all credit cards combined.

Alexander King

A graduate of the University of Moral Stupidity. He finished magna cum nutty! A brilliant, cynical, wonderful man.

Kiss

Tough on chapped lips . . . thrilling to lippy chaps.

Kiss

Two divided by nothing . . .
The pressure was all mine.

The two auricular oris muscles in juxtaposition and in a state of contraction . . . I do believe it is more than that.

Kitchen

Where the woman's brain is cooked.
As much Christian activity takes place there as in a pulpit.

L

Laziness

Work for a busy person; the chief sapper of energy known . . . goal for retirees . . . hyper activity for the dead.

Archibald Leach. . . .

. . is an eminent authority on the origin of man. He should be; after all, he has studied all his life to be an actor. A few earthlings know this scholar as Cary Grant.

I am told that he believes the moon craters were made by bombs. Centuries have passed since moon people destroyed their planet by some form of explosive.

Some few people escaped to earth—so, here we are.

Now we are attempting to go to the moon to discover an escape hatch to which we can flee when the earth craters are formed by hydrogen bombs. I am quite sure that the real reason young lovers look to the moon is that basically man is a homing pigeon and these pie-eyed young people are merely expressing a maternal fixation on good old mother moon.

When they marry, I wonder where they will go on their honeyearth?

Leadership

The difference between a leader and others is that a leader organizes his ideas in such a fashion that the rest of us are challenged by the fact that he knows so much about the subject we are willing to follow him in the quest. This is true if the quest seems to have merit.

A leader can say in words that which sums up the frustrations, hopes and beliefs all of us have been feeling; thus, he incarnates within himself the promise of fulfillment and we follow him.

Often a leader is disillusioned by the fact that those younger or older than he admire and follow him but his contemporaries never seem willing to forgive him for success. This is most strange because the success of a contemporary indicates that one's age has arrived.

Contemporaries ought to cheer most. They seldom do.

A leader is one who can face a massive problem, break it into small bits of work which, when each bit is accomplished, brings the whole group that much nearer the ultimate goal.

A true leader must be humble. This will make it possible for him to listen with patience to the various views reflected by every segment of his supporters, to attempt to effect homogeneiety of mutually exclusive and hostile-to-each-other groups, and to forge a new path of action in direct opposition to suggestions of some of his most ardent friends who see a part and mistake it for the whole.

The leader's verse is James 1:19. "Be swift to hear, slow to speak, slow to wrath."

The more of the whole group the leader can carry forward, the better leader he is. A good leader is tested by how few he leaves behind.

A leader soon discovers that he who will not follow and cannot lead invariably obstructs. The greatest test of the metal of a leader is how he handles such people.

The leader who sees a part and mistakes it for the whole always misdirects. The leader who sees the whole and mistakes it for a part always delays.

There are two sorts of opposition: he who honestly yet lovingly disagrees, and he who disagrees because of psychic reaction to the leader's personality.

Usually the first can be dealt with by further information; the second will never be satisfied until the leader has been removed.

74

The leader must neither allow the second type to have reason to further dislike him nor be put in a position to obstruct the leader's program—because he will surely try.

Read Robert St. Claire's *Neurotics In The Church* for a thorough analysis of the second type.

This group is the greatest inhibitor to the Kingdom of God. They are always unhappy. The leader should remind them that the door is open for them to return, that he respects them—but he should beware of giving them too much rein too soon.

Leadership

I completely disagree with a cliché of our time. It should read "too many Indians; not enough chiefs."

Lengthy Sermon

The ecclesiastical equivalent of the fifty mile hike. The mind can absorb no more than the seat can endure.

Lenin

Ross Coggins reports that every two weeks Lenin's tomb is closed for 24 hours so Lenin's body can receive a special cleaning process. This is probably due to the fact that the Russians don't want to wash their dirty Lenin in public.

Oscar Levant

He is so ill I marvel that he is able to stand. Come to think of it, I haven't seen him stand since 1948. His is the most animated corpse I have ever seen.

John L. Lewis

The Ugly American. I would clip his eyebrows for fifty percent of everything I found in them. A great orator, akin to the Hebrew Prophets.

Liberal-Conservative

The liberals seem to be at sea; the conservatives seem so angry. Neither is appealing.

Life's Formula for Success

Beginning from childhood give ten percent of your gross income to God; save ten percent of your gross income; always do ten percent more than those over you ask or expect of you, and you will be such a success that you will be an employer before you are 35, independent at 45, and able to retire (but don't do it) at 55.

Light

What you need more of if you need a sun tan or inspiration. In my first pastorate, old Brother Siegler would say, "We need more light." I never knew if he was referring to our gas lamps or me. I think I know which.

The Lord's Supper

The most holy experience of love for Jesus Christ. I have trembled and wept as I served it. A dynamic symbol.

Love

There are two kinds of love in the world. Love type #1: I love you because you are of value to me in the realm of sex, fame, ambition fulfillment or as a complement to personality. When you lose these characteristics, I love you no longer. This is pagan love.

Love type #2: I love you whether you are of value to me or not. My love for you lies in my heart—not in your value. This is Christian love.

Lovelessness

The old toothless woman limber lipped the words to me. "Them doctors diagnosed Maudie's death one way but they was dead wrong. What she really passed on of was *the pure neglects.*"

Lubbock, Texas

If someone should send me a quart of Lubbock dirt, I believe I would put it on my cereal each morning. Very high fluoride, you know. Besides, I'm sometimes homesick.

During one of their sandstorms I saw a prairie dog digging 37½ feet in the air.

When I was living in Littlefield, it rained in Lubbock. Our car was in the garage so we didn't get to see it.

Douglas MacArthur

A far greater man than the people who kept him from the presidency. If he said he kept himself from the presidency, he was greater than himself.

Man

A more or less efficient design several thousand years old. It has been able to cope with temperature control, city traffic, the saber toothed tiger, governmental control, but has never been able to regulate his passion and temper. If man is incapable of producing some ecological system for maintenance of balance in personality, he can now eliminate himself.

Christ offers to save him from extinction. Will this civilized neurotic called man follow the sandaled feet or not?

Man

Dog's best friend. Privileged primate—will be extinct in the next 1000 years, due to overpopulation, dehydration, and rape of the sod. His only hope is Jesus Christ, whose object of love is man.

Manufacture

I honestly believe the modern manufacturer can predict within sixty days of when a certain part will become faulty. Built-in obsolescence is necessary to keep up the economy, they tell us. In other words our economy is based on inferiority rather than quality.

Can this be interpreted as anything other than immortality?

Carlyle Marney

A former trombonist now preaching in Charlotte. He once said, "Modern man is as mixed up as a termite in a yo-yo." A really brilliant analyst of human theatrics.

Angel Martinez

A very effective preacher and close friend of many years. One of my favorite stories about Angel took place many years ago when he was a very young ministerial student at Baylor University. They had taken Angel out of San Antonio but they had not taken San Antonio out of Angel.

He simply loved to eat Mexican red hots, chili peques. He had been eating them all his life and ate them like peanuts.

After dinner in the home of a Deacon, Angel ate a few of the little balls of fire. The Deacon noticed it and asked for a handful of them, assuring Angel he could eat anything the young minister could. The Deacon swallowed about a dozen of them . . .

. . . Three gallons of water later, the flaming Deacon exclaimed, "I've heard many preachers preach about Hell; but you are the first one I've ever known who carried samples with him!"

Marxism

Such a ridiculous idea that within fifty years it will be an historic hangover. It will bury itself.

Roy O. McClain

The only minister about whom people are asking the same question they ask about Jack Paar: "What is Roy McClain really like?"

Meditation

The motionless exercise that gets me out of the way so the forces of God can move through my personality when it returns to expression.

Metrecal

Cause of the Incredible Shrinking Man or the Vanishing American.

Mimeograph Machine

An instrument of the devil.

Minister

The most precarious position known to man. The average pastor is faced with a congregation of truly great saints plus half a dozen neurotics. If one neurotic really gets after the pastor, the congregation will reluctantly side with the sick person. It is not long after such experience the pastor moves to another field of service.

This is the reason we could be living in the post-Protestant era.

Every person interested in this terrible problem should read Robert James St. Clair's *Neurotics in the Church*.

The hope of our nation rests in pastors who will buck this condition fearlessly and congregations that will manifest enough maturity to side with the minister.

The churches that have shown this equibalance have been blessed beyond belief.

Misnomer

Nine-year-old boy in Glorieta, New Mexico: "Let's sing that song about Alfred and Omega."

Missions

If God wills the evangelization of the world and you are not interested in missions, you are opposing the will of God.

What right have you to hear the gospel twice when there are millions who have never heard it once?

Mistakes

Architects cover their mistakes with paint; doctors with sod; brides with mayonnaise; and hypocrites with ritual.

Mom, Dad, and Sister Jeanne

Dad had two heads, so did Mom. When they met, it was love at fourth sight. They got married so they could share a four-way cold tablet. I'll bet you really and truly thought I was serious about Mom and Dad's two heads. Now, don't try to deny it—I bet you really thought I was serious.

Well, I was.

I honestly do recall seeing my father at the lunch table with his hat on his head, a telephone on his ear, a cigar in his mouth, munching his food.

"I'm in a hurry," he explained.

We gathered.

My eyesight has never been exceptional. When I was a student at Baylor University, Dr. Tidwell, the great professor of Bible, challenged us to find someone, anyone, and talk to him about Christ.

My friend, Bill Betts, loved to tell about finding me, Bible in hand, witnessing to a barber pole.

My poor eyesight must stem from heredity plus the fact that when I was an infant, mother played the piano for the silent movies. There I was in my little crib, four feet from that brilliant, giant screen, trying to focus on the unfocusable. Everytime Francis X. Bushman hugged Mary Pickford, they mashed my little already pointed head. With all that pushing and shoving going on, the old nude stringed piano pounding in my ears, and the 2000 candlepower screen blazing into my baby blue bloodshot orbs, it is a miracle that I am not a blind, deaf mongoloid.

For the first two years of my life each of my eyes were on different Sundays looking toward Wednesday. People look at most babies and exclaim, "How precious!" When the old time, plain spoken West Texans looked at me, they would say flatly, "Pore thang—you think it'll live?"

My sister, Jeanne, is a wonderfully dedicated Christian girl of seventeen. If this book is printed, she will have much to overcome.

My father was associated with various people in the carnival business for many years. His bible for twenty years was *The Billboard.*

Long before I became interested in Christian work and knew anything about the Bible or the church, I knew such edifying words as fink, darb, lop, lum, l. g., fuzz and rag bag. Shortly after I learned a little English, I was taught to speak "Kissarney Lissingo."

My dad's philosophy of money was rather interesting. Wishing to teach me the finer ways of life, he would look me in the eye, speak endearingly with a tear in his voice, and say, "Son, you can't run a business on toilet paper. It takes the long green."

Monday

If salvation were to depend on feeling and if Christ came back to the earth on Monday, all preachers would go to hell.

The day I feel that I have greeted the dawn by gargling with window putty.

On Monday when I am at my best I am "up to porely."

The day I have to make a massive leap to touch a snake's navel.

My headache day. I would take an alka seltzer but I can't stand the noise.

Money

More money is wasted, more great work is ruined, and more precious time is lost by seeking to get the lowest price. I wish I had a dollar worth $.75.

Marilyn Monroe

Did not kill herself. She destroyed the person the image makers had made her become, so it was murder—not suicide. She is the only person in history who killed herself and someone else at the same time.

Month

To the cynic large segment of boredom divided into thirty units.

Jess Moody, Sr.

My grandfather, for whom I was named, was a really unusual character.

The favorite family story concerning Jess Moody dates back to 1918. He was selling an ice cold orange drink at a county fair. This inticing beverage he called "Dr. Moody's Health Drink."

The opening day at the fair involved a ribbon cutting by the local dignitaries. The entrance to the fair was on a hill about 200 yards from the little open air stand that dispensed that happy elixir which was really nothing but sweet orange colored water.

At least 5,000 people would come charging down the hill as soon as the ribbon was cut.

Just before the host of humanity made its descent upon Dr. Moody's Health Stand, a posse of cowboys came thundering by Dad Moody's happy business opportunity, filling the air with dust. When it settled, the giant vat containing Dr. Moody's Health Drink was filled with dust, straw, etc. (You should have seen what was in the etcetera.)

My father and his twin brother, Pete, who were then 16, moved swiftly to solve the problem of purifying the corrupted potion before the Great Opportunity passed them by.

Dad told grandfather to remove his clothes. Without a question he stripped to the altogether. Pete and Dad stretched his long handles over the top of a new vat and strained Dr. Moody's Health Drink through Granddad's underwear. This process of sanitation removed the debris, including the etcetera, thus dramatically saving the day and earning a yard and a half ($150.00—for the unenlightened) through the sale of this boon to mankind: Dr. Moody's Health Drink.

Walter Moore

Walter Moore loves to tell about the man who told Billy Sunday, "If you will tell me where Cain got his wife, I'll believe your Gospel."

Sunday snapped back, "You won't be the first man who went to hell worrying about another man's wife."

Morals

Improved impulses.

Mormons

If you think the population explosion is a problem now, here's something to think about. What if the Ecumenical Council results in a merger of the Roman Catholics and the Mormons?

Mosquito

Like a child—when silent one knows he's in something.

Muleshoe, Texas

The citizens of this acknowledged culture center are planning to erect a monument to a mule that brays every hour. Imagine walking down the street and hearing the ear splitting blast of the braying of one of these intelligent beasts and saying, "My goodness, it's one o'clock!"

My Contribution to World Peace
(or Humility and How I Attained It)

When I was ten I began to exercise my mind as to what I should do in life. At first I decided to discover America but later rejected the thought on the grounds that it would not be very original.

I forthwith made up my mind to sail around the Magellan Straits—but then I discovered why they called it the Magellan Straits.

There was no originality in doing what that man Magellan had had the foresight to do ahead of me.

This act of his certainly took the desire out of me to sail around the Magellan Straits. In fact it made me so angry that I vowed never to go near the Magellan Straits. That would show Mr. Magellan how I felt about it.

And, you know, it may be hard for you to believe, but I have kept my word until this very hour. I intend to keep my word until the day I die and never darken those Straits with my presence.

There would be only one way I could be enticed into going around the Magellan Straits . . . and that would be if it would help somebody.

If someone *really needed* for me to go I would swallow my pride and do it.

Then I decided to free the slaves—but there, standing in my way, was—guess who?—Abraham Lincoln.

Always someone stands in my way.

No matter where I turn there stands a Columbus, Magellan, or Lincoln. It is getting so there is hardly any room for greatness anymore. Always somebody reminds me that it's been done before. I'm tired of Columbus, Magellan, and Lincoln shoving me around.

This is why little guys like me never get anything much done.

We're frustrated.

Yessir, we're frustrated, I said.

Why?

Easy.

Just because some Columbus gets put in the world before we do, he takes advantage of us and up and discovers America without ever giving us a chance to do it.

Unfair!

Maybe others have not spoken up before but the time for redress of grievances has come and the Constitution guarantees it, so I want it!

Millions of little people have resented this Columbus intrusion through the centuries but have been afraid to speak.

They are the ones I call the smoldering masses.

That's who they are.

I'll speak up for them.

Only I.

They talk about equality of opportunity. Tell it to the Marines! And if they are busy somewhere doing good for the country, tell it to somebody else.

But tell it, friend.

I'll tell you what let's do.

Let's form a conspiracy against all these Columbus type people. Let's make up our minds *not* to be great. There are very few great things left to do due to the thoughtless self seeking of these Magellans.

But there are a few.

Let's make up our minds not to do them.

I know what I will not do.

I will square my jaw and refuse to discover the cure for cancer.

How's that!

I won't use up one good solid place in history. I'll leave the discovery of the cure for cancer to some struggling young man who really *needs* to discover the cure for cancer.

I'll be big about it. I won't push and shove my way around the history books. Columbus, Magellan, and Lincoln may have done it, but not me.

No.

My place in history will consist in the fact that out of the greatness of my heart and the humility of my soul, I left it up to the other person.

I'm the one who gave *all* the little smolderers a chance to conflagrate.

That's right, friend, *me.*

I, Jess Moody, of West Palm Beach, Florida—I did it out of my own free will.

I did it.

And nobody else, that's who.

I'm the one who really let George do it.

O. K., George, get to work—and you are welcome.

Think nothing of it.

Only one request, George.

When the cameras are flashing, the reporters are crowding you with questions, think of me.

I am sure a tear will wend its way down your cheek and you will quietly say, "If it weren't for Jess Moody of West Palm Beach, Florida, I wouldn't be here. All that I am and all that I hope to be, I owe to this, my angel brother."

I can hear Norman Vincent Price, the New York Cardinal, speak from his pulpit, "Moody the Humble, refused glory and fame so Arronson G. Lindbladt could be the discoverer of the Cure. Let us all vow to follow his example and not do great things either. Soon all will refuse to be great, in honor preferring one another. This will cause universal peace."

Dr. Price will continue, "Most of the trouble in the world is caused by competitive struggling for greatness. They talk of the Lonely Top. This kind of cooperation will make it even more lonely—and more selfish. Instead of the Lonely Top, let us not forget Moody and his Crowded Bottom!"

The congregation will love Dr. Vincent for that sermon, I'll bet you.

N

A National Mourner's Bench

We are not really a thoughtful people. Even our leaders seem to be able to look in only one direction at a time.

An example is the assassination of John F. Kennedy. When he came to Texas, the press said if he had any trouble it would be from the Right, the Conservatives.

While everyone was looking to the Right, the bullet came from the Left.

The death of our young president should have caused leaders of Left and Right to come together and say, "Look, let's stop this personal in-fighting! The death of President Kennedy has taught us the danger of personifying our hatred. From this day on we will mutually respect each other and deal only with the issues, their merits and demerits."

Wouldn't this have been a healing balm for our House of Sorrow?

What maturity have we gained from this national tragedy? None.

In fact, if anything, we are more neurotic than ever.

The Left accuses the Right of being character assassins.

But has not the Left pulled as many verbal triggers against the leaders of the Right as the Right against the Left?

Do not our journalists see how much dirt can be dug up on the leaders of both wings in order to print a juicy story?

Who deals with issues these days?

Everyone of these areas of tension, instead of being dynamically creative, producing thoughtful well balanced decisions, has produced mistrust of brother men, venom, accusations, and pure undistilled Hate.

The Man of Nazareth must weep as He sees His children acting with less maturity than we had twenty years ago.

When will we see that hate is not a characteristic of a political philosophy, a section of the country, or a color of the skin?

Hate is a result of something much deeper than these surface manifestations. Hate is the result of sin.

The only cure for sin is forgiveness from God.

Uncle Sam needs to kneel at the Mourner's Bench . . . he'd better do it soon . . .

. . . lest our problem be not integration, but disintegration.

> The Left curses the Right,
> The Negro blames the White,
> The Gentile hates the Jew,
> Labor fights Management,
> And I hate you!

Negro

Though my earliest years were spent in an environment completely intolerant of the Negro, I have felt no prejudice whatsoever toward my friends of that or any other race.

When I understood that in spite of the fact that Jesus was of another race and another color (carpenters in His day were nearly black), and that He died for me, a white man, I could not entertain the slightest tinge of racism.

The highest compliment I ever received—or at least the one that most touched my heart—was from a good colored friend in Owensboro, Kentucky. When I informed him that I was leaving my pastorate, a tear shone on his cheek as he said, "Dr. Moody, you just can't go. Why, you are pastor of every colored person in this town."

I had to hurry away.

I have never worked with a colored person whom I did not love and respect; I believe they have felt the same way.

New Mexico

There are just two times when I like that state: When I am awake and when I am asleep. At all other times I just can't stand it.

New Orleans

A city in Louisiana. That's all a minister can say about it.

Nightclub

A sottish, sociological septic tank where the bored bore the bores in a vicious cycle unto cynicism.

The Ninth Stone

When a person is accused of some deviation from social custom, of course it should be dealt with by the Crowd.

The efforts of the crowd are always swift and infinitely effective. You waste no time and money with this method. You can stand democratically with the Group.

But don't be pushy about it.

Be a good follower. If others want to lead out, let them.

Don't cast the first stone. The good Lord forbade that.

Cast the eighth or ninth stone.

This way you won't be blamed in case there is a slight error in the Crowd judgment. It's the first stoners who go to jail and are vilified by the unjust courts.

Very few First Stoners remain in circulation for long.

They are usually framed by the police and sent away.

But I never heard of a Ninth Stoner who received even so much as a rebuff from anybody.

You can be a Ninth Stoner all your life and never have your integrity questioned.

I know many of them who do very well for themselves. A very good friend of mine lives in suburbia, has a lovely home, a beautiful wife, and two fine sons. He is a leader in his community, his lodge, his church.

He is always saying wise things like, "Where there's smoke there's fire . . ." . . . or, "One accuser might be wrong, but fifty—never!"

He must be in the right because his conscience never disturbs him. If a mistake is made it is made by the First Stoner. The Ninth Stoner can't be too much awry in his estimation of things.

If he is wrong there have been eight errors in judgment ahead of him.

And he is not without courage. Think how the Fifteenth Stoner must look up to him.

I heard a Fifteenth Stoner, with admiration bursting out all over him, say, "Man, old 'X' really stands up to them. I don't call what he has courage, I call it guts."

To repeat what I said before. He must be in the right. His conscience doesn't disturb him.

They say he sleeps like a rock—and with one.

Richard Nixon

Wha' happen?

94

O

Others

It took the combined efforts of a million people to put one man in space.

In fact, it took quite a host of intercooperating people to make it possible for me to sit down to breakfast this morning.

The chair and the table were made by North Carolinians, the dishes were handed me by New Englanders, and my silver was given me by helping hands from Sheffield.

My coffee was brewed by a Brazilian, my sugar was spooned for me by a Louisianian, and the cream was poured by a Florida dairyman.

A Californian made my jelly, a Georgian my butter, a Texan my bacon, and a neighbor's Methodist hen my eggs.

I am indebted to most of the United States and several foreign countries before I rise from the breakfast table.

Who said "I am the master of my fate?"

P

Jack Paar

A good catalyst who alternates between the most incredible maturity and the most unbelievable adult tantrums. I like him because I see myself in him.

Pacifism

Synonym for appeasement and lack of character. Probably caused more wars than militarism.

Vance Packard

Writes in black ink on dark wrapping paper at midnight from the bottom of a cave and makes a handsome living out of it. You call this the "power of negative thinking."

Palm Beach

The world's most elegant little island. It is a place that will fool you. Understand one fact and you have the key to interpreting this city. If you see someone extremely well dressed, a sartorial splendor—he is not one of the wealthy residents. But if you see

someone who appears to be a bum, attired in the most bedraggled
garb imaginable—lo, he is not one of them either.

Parents

A blessing and a curse.
Loved when needed.
An unpaid lecturer.
The waiter, the porter, the upstairs maid.
A human mint.
A cousin to cornucopia.

Pastor

Community sponge who soaks in problems. He soaks until he
croaks.
Must have the heart of a lamb and the hide of a rhinocerous.
Not the simpleton Hollywood has depicted him to be—probably the most aware person in the community. He lives with the
Bible, great books, and human heartbreak.
Some of the greatest evidences of courage I have witnessed have
been manifested by these men who march to the sound of a
different drummer. I wish I were more like most of them. I have
seen many of them crucified because of their courage to rebuke
institutionalized evil.
If Hollywood wants some real drama, I can personally tell them
some great stories about Gospel gumption.

Norman Vincent Peale

A singularly great man who is plagued by weak mimics. It isn't Peale—it is his "pealings." In the first century Paul was appealing. In the twentieth century Peale is appalling.

Actually, Dr. Peale is one of America's most helpful people.

Peanut Butter

I 'ike it but it gets stuck on the 'oof of my mouth. Used by autotaxidermists.

Pennies

Train up a child to give pennies and when he is old he will not depart from it.

Perseverance

If your faith fizzles before the finish it was faulty from the first.

Phonograph Record

Ear wax.
Today's flattery—tomorrow's embarrassment.

Pie

My taste buds haven't changed so greatly since I was a child. The fact is that pies are not as good as they once were. I would give $3.61 for one piece of pie as delicious as those I inhaled as a boy.

Whoever scuttled this art should be liquidated by drowning in insipid modern pie dough.

Plots

The movies are producing such extravaganzas that about the only plot left is . . . . a man and woman in orbit in a single capsule. The earth below engages in a thermonuclear war and every person is eliminated. They make their descent to repeat the whole Human Affair. His name is Atom. Hers is Evil. The title could be, "Not Again!"

If Arthur Miller were writing it, the plot would really thicken when the two get in a hassel over the one remaining fig leaf—and decide to get a divorce.

His title would be "Now What?" He would probably end it with a very frustrated amoeba in a tropical swamp saying, "O, well, here I go again."

Just then a huge branch begins to fall on the amoeba.

We are never told what happens.

We will be haunted by the question, "Did the amoeba split in time? Come back in 70 million years to see."

This would be one movie longer than "Gone With The Wind."

Point

That which most people never get to.
That which one does to get others to concentrate elsewhere.
Active Inferiority.

Politician

There are too many morons manipulating the nation's marbles in a game called "keeps." A politican thinks of the next election; a statesman thinks of the next generation.

Politicians

If one could go to the moon by gas, many of them would have been there long ago.

The Population Explosion . . .

. . . among dogs is becoming one of our greatest problems. The dog population of the United States is twenty seven million. (Oops! It is more than that now.) This is a 250 per cent increase in the last three decades.

I'm appealing to the scientific world to come up with a birth control bone for dogs.

And what about a course in sex education for dogs at the training school? This is a whole new field of investigation.

I realize that the Roman Catholic puppies might raise a question about it. But an interfaith Council could convene and come up with an intelligent formula for action, which would be palatable to the more pious pups.

Some plan needs to be worked out that will be acceptable to all dogs regardless of race, collar, or breed.

Leslie Porter

The Nathan Porters have two vivacious little daughters, Beka and Leslie. Mrs. Porter noticed that Leslie had a rather badly infected finger.

"Leslie, you are rotting away," she said with concern.

"Yes, Mother," said the moppet, "and I don't want to go."

Positive Thinking

The ball player who stands on third and thinks positively about scoring will never get home. It takes legs that churn like pistons.

Faith and legs equal a stolen base.

Posthumous Glory

At twenty, I knew I would go down in history. Now I know I'll just go down.

Maturity is best measured by how a man accepts posthumous anonymity.

Who goes out to see a grave marker these days?

Poverty

During the depression we were the poor people the poor people called poor people.

Practical Joke

An impractical thing to do.

Preaching

Soul communication. Every minister should make a pulpit a miniature Calvary where he dies a little for his people . . . sometimes a battle between leather lungs and wooden ears. It is a sad sight to see a congregation, like a storm tossed schooner, blow out of the sanctuary in a mad rush to beat the Methodists to the cafeteria. Then one little lady comes to the minister and drones, ". . . enjoyed your little talk."

Prejudice

A method of making disposition of a painful reality by predisposition. From the word prejudge. To prejudge is to judge anything without contemplation upon the facts. Anytime we act without complete evaluation of the facts, we are prejudiced.

Prescription

Why is it that the prescription is illegible but the doctor's bill is clear as day?

The Presence . . .

. . . of Christ changes any external situation into a glory.

When Bishop Selwyn was cast into a pig pen by his persecutors, he changed it into an altar of worship.

John Nelson was imprisoned under a slaughterhouse. It stank worse than imagination can conjure, as blood and filth flowed into the warm, foul dungeon. The Presence of Christ made it a paradise of love to him.

Didn't John Bunyan make the vermin infested Bedford Jail his Palace Beautiful?

I Am Nominated President of the United States

A tragicomedy could be written about what goes on in a pastor's study. I know of no arena of activity more surcharged with drama, pathos, humor and cynicism.

I have been visited by Baptist Balzacs, who report every lewd and lurid thing taking place in the city. Then there are the big bunch of bats who swarm in to get the minister to solve the chief sociological evils with some spiritual woofle dust. Nymphomaniacs, frustrates, neurotics, lesbians, homosexuals, doubters, double dealers, hypocrites, soul searchers, con men come wanting a one visit, no responsibility holy hypo from the minister. Others honestly on the rocks wanting to be shown and helped down the road back.

I could write a ten volume set about the visitors to my study.

This particular story concerns a truly great moment in my life.

My secretray, Miss Banks, informed me that Mrs. D_____ wanted to see me. I recognized the name as belonging to a voice that belonged to a woman who had called several times to inform me of a very important document in her possession which she had to reveal to me "because I can trust you."

Let me digress a tad to describe my office. I suppose it is a rather typical modern minister's study. I have bedecked it with a few mementoes and doodads which I treasure. Miniature statues of Moses, Francis of Assisi, and Don Quixote teach me to lead the people according to God's will and with courage as Moses; to love the people and be gentle as Francis of Assisi; and not to go off on wild, fanciful crusades as did Don Quixote.

There are also some pictures in my office: Winston Churchill, photographed by Maurice Holley from our congregation; Sammy Snead and I when "I gave him a golf lesson;" R. G. Smith, an old cowboy friend of mine now in heaven; R. G. Lee, the great orator; Billy Graham and I in Miami; and the President and Billy Graham.

It was the last picture that did it.

Mrs. D_____ came into the office, a heavy manila envelope under her arm, her plumage flying, and a look of destiny and mission about her—a sixty-five-year old overstuffed, undermartyred Joan of Arc.

She sat down directly in front of me, dreadnaughtlike. I gave her the usual quiet assurances that any matter she presented to me would be guarded as a treasure not to be mentioned to the congregation, or anyone.

Mrs. D_____ was calm enough at first, then she looked at my wall. First she saw President Kennedy and stiffened; then Billy Graham.

That did it.

She leaped to her feet and shouted "Glory t' God in the Highest! I have never seen so much destiny wrapped up in one room. I have come for such an hour as this!"

She wheeled on her heels and shouted in my face, "Boy, sit up!!!"

I became rigid as month old hay bread.

"You've wondered what I have in this envelope, haven't you? I can tell by your face."

I didn't know it showed.

"Well, it is enough facts—not fiction—facts, boy, facts to send the President to the electric chair! Enough information to blast him out of office."

I was sure Mr. Goldwater would have given a department store for those precious documents.

"Now, I have a master plan, a plan that will save America. I will expose the President; and, of course, he will be removed from office . . ." Somehow I felt for him.

". . . . Then we will nominate and elect with the greatest landslide in history the next President of the United States, Mr. Billy Graham!"

I was thrilled to death at the thought.

"Now, Jess C. Moody, Pastor of the First Baptist Church of West Palm Beach, get your fanny out of that chair. . . ."

I started to rise.

". . . . Get up, leave this job that pays you peanuts and go to your destiny, boy, because you are to be nominated and elected by a landslide the next Vice President of the United States!!"

"Only Vice President?" I questioned, disappointment written all over me.

A few days later, another triumphal entry was made. Mrs. D____ was back in my study where I was still holding down my peanut job.

"Boy! I heard you stand in the prow of the Chapel-By-The-Lake last night. I have never heard such a sermon. You mortally preached! Now brace yourself . . ."

I braced.

"I've been thinking this thing through. Now, don't be shocked. Don't faint. After preaching that marvelous message, I have decided to *eliminate* Billy Graham. The next president of the United States will be Jess Moody!"

I could have cried for joy.

Then Mrs. D____ seemed to be transformed into an angel of

light. She was really wheeling now. She leaped into a chair, towering over me. I didn't dare move. She looked around the room, like Napoleon surveying the troops.

"Listen to them cheer, Boy, listen!" She then signalled for the throng to quieten.

They must have quietened because she raised her stentorian voice to a politician's roar.

"My fellow Republicans," she thundered, "We all know why we are here. There is no standing doubt about our nominee."

Certainly not, I was sitting.

"My nominee hails from . . . from . . . where abouts you from, boy?," she whispered in an aside from the crowd.

"Near Muleshoe, Texas," I whispered back. She looked sick as a bloodhound. Obviously, I could hail from a greater vote getting center than that.

Undaunted she turned back to her audience. "My candidate is from a small Texas town . ."

I was sorry she didn't give Muleshoe a plug. Lord knows, they need it.

She continued this din of ear crucifixion for a few minutes, then with a flourish she climaxed her nomination speech with this choice morsel.

"Of whom else could I be speaking but Jess B. Moody!"

In spite of the fact that my middle initial is "C," I knew I was in after that speech.

She leaped from the chair and paraded about the room in a victory march.

"Up, boy, up—to your destiny!"

I got up and marched with her until we came by my office door and into the outer office the hosts tramped.

I sagged exhausted into the chief seat of the peanut business.

It was good to be back.

Problems

We handle every problem in one of three ways, according to my friend, Dr. Donald Robertson: fight, flight, or make a deal.

Progress

Our fathers resolved issues more efficiently than we seem able to do. Our day seems to be riding a bicycle with no chain.

Many of us can recall the tolerated squalor of poor houses and insane asylums, the beating of strikers and circulation of blacklists, the unrestricted business monopolies, woman and child labor, the squandering of natural resources, poor sanitation, unchecked corruption, collusions and connivances of state and local governments. The immediate past generation did some pretty effective work on these moral blights.

The difference between then and now seems to be that then the social reformers dealt with issues. Today we attempt to neutralize our opposition by hurling epithets at the person who symbolizes the opposing view. We are so occupied with name calling that we have little time left to deal with the issues at hand.

And we're not even very creative in our name calling. I'm getting a little bored with the noncreative title tossing.

Can't we think of anything but *communist, fascist, Ku Kluxer or pinko?*

Both left and right are going to lose because they will bore us to death.

He who slings mud is losing ground fast.

As one not so bright said very brightly the other day—"Gollee, it looks like we are progressing into obscurity."

Prohibition

I once had a donkey friend (I have had several friends who were donkeys). One day he met a flea who was quite a promoter and his miniature manipulator evoked an agreement from the donkey to this effect: The flea would become a resident of the donkey's back and for every quart of blood the flea took from him he would return a thimbleful as revenue.

The donkey bought the proposition. Soon, for some reason, the donkey sickened and finally died.

But why should I report such a story to you? This couldn't happen to us . . . . because only a Jackass would fall for an economy like that.

As Will Rogers said, "We must have the revenue to pave the highways so the Baptists can go to the conventions."

Prophet

Not a sacred sourpuss, but an accurate analyst who observes the cracks in the ground promising a forthcoming sociological earthquake.

Psyche

Rusted psyches are barometers of the dampness of the soul.

Psychiatrist

A good psychiatrist is one who shrinks your head while enlarging your heart.

My psychiatrist says I have a persecution complex, but he only says that because he hates me.

Q

Quiet

The loudest noise known to man. Becoming a most rare commodity these days.

If used in proper perspective and mixed with prayer and spiritual dedication, the result can be the formula for soul revolution.

Our more noisy, aggressive denominations need periods of great quietude and our more quiet denominations need to increase the decibels and raise more holy heaven, sans red faced bigotry.

This would blow out our spiritual sinuses and the ecclesiastical cobwebs that may have accumulated in our zeal chamber.

For the loud to shut up and the quiet to speak up would do us all a heap of good.

R

Rain

A service station attendant from Santa Rosa, New Mexico was asked if it rained much in Santa Rosa.

"Yes, the Bible records the story of the only rain Santa Rosa ever had. It was when the great flood covered the whole earth. They say when that happened, Santa Rosa got half an inch."

Raising Money

If churches would expend as much energy winning men to Christ as they do raising money, they would have no monetary problems.

Bob Randall

One of the finest Christian pianists I know. While we were conducting a preaching mission in London's Peckham Rye, Bob played "The Battle Hymn of the Republic" just before I spoke. The only problem was that the British knew it only as "John Brown's Body."

When we were in services in Edinburgh, Bob played "The Ninety and Nine" on the little organ on which Ira Sankey composed the hymn. When Bob played only one verse, I asked why he didn't play more. I won't forget his breathless answer. "To pedal that little organ was like riding a bicycle with square wheels in mud up to your waist."

Sam Rayburn

The most villainous appearing good man I ever knew. A Christian gentleman.

Recipe

Mix lemon juice with orange peelings (thoroughly grated) until it forms a rather thick substance. Add sugar—mix thoroughly and stir with a wooden fork. Sprinkle just a dash of cinnamon.

As soon as it has reached just the right consistency, immediately throw it out the window, put on your coat, drive to Schraft's and eat their delicious cheese souffle.

Record

That which inspires champions and gave me a double hernia. A reminder of mass mediocrity.

Republican

The modern Republican is nothing but a slow Democrat.

Rest

What some people use to store up rambunctiousness for future hellishness.

Retreat

I sometimes want to retreat from my multitudinous duties for a highly specialized, seldom taxing responsibility . . . . something like being a Baptist Bishop to Bothered Buddhists on Boston's Beacon Street.

Eddie Rickenbacker

I met him at Hunt, Texas, near his fabulous ranch in the deer country.

I never knew a man who was successful in any venture who didn't have a formula.

I asked Mr. R. as to what he attributed his success.

His answer is worth considering: "Timing and courage."

Oral Roberts

Everytime I see him on TV, I can almost hear the good Lord say "Please, Oral, I'd rather do it myself!"

I believe in divine healing. I'm not sure I believe in divine healers.

Will Rogers

I am related to Will Rogers and very proud of it. Many people *claim* kinship to Will, no matter how distant the real or imagined relationship.

I don't have to strain to find my kinship to him. You see, he was my grandmother's aunt's cousin's twin brother's uncle's son-in-law by marriage twice removed by divorce on his father's daughter's nephew on his grandmother's side and she rode a bicycle.

Seriously, my maternal forebearers were Schrimscher's from Oklahoma. Will Rogers' mother was a Schrimsher. All the Schrimschers from Oklahoma are closely related.

When I was introduced to Will Rogers one month before he died, he just smiled at me and patted my little head. This was July 4, 1935 at Stamford, Texas during the Texas Cowboy Reunion.

There are many of Will's quotes which I will long remember, but the one I remember most is what he said to me, "Son, get off my shoes!"

That hot dusty day at the rodeo, I must have really pushed my way up close. He finally shook hands with me.

I didn't wash that hand for six weeks after I shook hands with Will.

Come to think of it, I hadn't washed it six weeks before I shook hands with him.

Bertrand Russell

A brilliant man who makes foolish statements when he is tired.

Russia

Bluff . . . excellent show window but the back of the store is burned out.

S

A Sabbath Day's Journey

Twice around the golf course.

If a minister played golf on Sunday, the Lord would allow him to make two holes-in-one. Wonderful! But whom could he tell?

When the Pastor is playing golf, he instructs his secretary to tell those who want to know his whereabouts: "You know the Greens? Well, he is visiting them."

A rabbi hits the golf ball and yells, "Three ninety-eight."

Saddle

Horse warmer . . . that which comes between the horse and the people, thus preventing understanding or oversitting. Seat of the great blister producing industry.

St. Vitus

The patron saint of the American people . . . what Uncle Philbert did when he mistook the itching powder for talcum.

Saxophone

Someone has called it "an ill wind that nobody blows any good."

If you are lost among the tall reeds, does this mean you can't find your way out of the bass sax section?

Scandal

A minister falls into moral evil; it is big news. God help the nation when it ceases to be.

Second Bathroom

Wife's other John. When your daughter marries, you don't lose a daughter you gain a bathroom.

The Second Coming

If there is no Second Coming of Christ, it is impossible to believe either in a moral universe or the character of God.

This is true because there must be some Cosmic Equalizer to vindicate the misrepresented, to reward the faithful, and to complete all knowledge.

If evil goes without ultimate punishment and good without ultimate reward, the result can only be final chaos.

Fanatics have distorted the story to such a degree that many have repudiated the whole idea, but why kill the goose because you don't like some of her feathers? It is not normal to repudiate the truth because of distortions in other realms, e. g. one doesn't do away with the good in liberal politics because there are hyper-liberals who advocate complete socialism; or do away with the character building qualities of a good conservatism because the hyperconservatives see a communist behind every progressive thought.

History does not move in cycles but a spiral, repeating and progressing. But progressing toward what—if not to a climax? All movement is toward something. What is the something toward which history journeys?

The Bible teaches that the something is the final curtain of history, climaxed by intervention of the Author just before the denouement.

The plot has become so involved by the ad libs and asides of the characters that only the Author can explain it and bring it to a conclusion. A comedy is a play in which the chief characters are confronted with a dilemma; and, through a series of events, overcome it.

A tragedy is a play in which the chief characters are confronted with a dilemma; and, through a series of events, are overcome by it.

When the Author steps on the stage of history . . . for some it will be a comedy, . . . for others it will be a tragedy.

This presently-realized-yet-to-happen event Christians call the Second Coming of Christ. What do pagans have to explain the purpose of men and nations?

The answer is, generally, nothing . . . . except beatnikism, libertinism, isolation and compassionless despair.

The Second Coming is the explanation of the superior ethics of Christians. A living eschatology coupled with the freesoulism of Eternal Security of the Christian makes for a very happy, non neurotic life . . .

. . . But throw the combination into imbalance and a weird non person is the result.

Eternal Security without eschatology results in epicurean antinomianism.

Eschatology without Eternal Security results in a stoical non social isolationism.

Separated, they are dangerous.

Together, they are dynamically good.

Secret

I can keep a secret; it is the people
I tell it to who can't.

Secretary

Should be able to think like a man, act like a lady, and work
like a horse. If you want a job well done, find a busy man, charge
him to do it. You'll see inspiration sweep over his face as he takes
the responsibility—then he will bravely give it to his secretary to
get it done.

All that I am and all that I hope to be I owe to my secretary.

Security

. . . Infinitely more dangerous than the atomic bomb. There
should be a massive program against the dangers of living without
tension. Flabby societies are failing societies. Once a people become accustomed to security, it is time for thinking men to begin
to seek out a new nation with a philosophy that will strike most
modern Americans as rather unique.

It is called "Little Government—Big People."

I am convinced that a democracy can live only until the people
discover that through taxation they can reach into the public
treasury and legislate themselves out of the kind of environment
that generates character and purpose.

The original purpose of this nation was an amoral government
and a moral people. Now we have an amoral people and a so-
called moral government. Actually, the moral government idea is
a rather obvious hypocrisy covering up vote getting hand out
programs. It is a repetition of bread and circuses to keep the
peasants quiet.

It is no coincidence, in my opinion, that the more socialistic a nation becomes, the less spiritually aware the people seem to be. I consider it no mere happenstance that the revival or evangelistic crusade is less desired by the church people now than twenty five years ago.

In this age of the all protecting national Big Brother, there is a rising contempt of the common decencies. Juvenile and parental delinquency is greater now than at any time in the history of our land. We spend more money on gambling than on national defense. An individual man or woman cannot safely walk at night down the streets or through the parks of our major cities.

The nation's capital has five hundred cocktail parties a day and is probably the most unsafe city in which to live, perhaps on the planet.

Seeds of mistrust are sown so that once friendly sectional rivalries have become deep seated hatreds. It is an unhappy time when special police guards have to be posted at intersectional football games.

We are a house of sad children when a thousand stores are robbed and devastated in three nights of rioting in only two American cities.

We are a hothouse of hatred when esteemed Negro ministers are called communists and kindly southerners are branded Ku Kluxers when they are unable to throw off generations of tradition in a few months time.

We are a home divided when Americans of liberal bent are branded as Moscow motivated and Americans of honest conservatism are derided as advocating the oxcart.

No generation has more reason to be as ashamed of itself as ours. We have lost our sense of humor, our sense of national purpose, and our sense of human respect.

It will take the analytical mind of Jefferson, the morality of Lee, the courage of Lincoln, and the robustness of Theodore Roosevelt to extricate us from our present controversial quicksand.

All of the best of our past must come forth now. The next generation must produce what the combination of our past generations have produced.

It is my conviction that there is only one way this can come about and that is through a God sent, Holy Spirit motivated revival. This cannot come about with cynical ministers, opportunistic politicians, imbalanced novelists, hot headed agitators and blind historians.

Selah

What David said when a harp string broke!

Self Criticism

Few people are very adept at this because anything takes repetitious practice.

Sense

It doesn't take much sense to get along in this world. All the sense it takes is sense enough to find someone who has some sense and get some sense from him.

Common sense is that sense without which sense all other sense is nonsense.

Sunrise

One of the big issues I face each day is why I should get out of bed this morning.

After all I have a big church and a beautiful wife. I should count my blessings. I should think about a minister friend of mine who has a beautiful church and a big wife.

Sermon

Mine are like the launching of a satellite: They begin with a roar, then I lose my head, and end up in the unknown.

The conveyance of eternal truth through a mere human being. The most solemn responsibility any man can have laid upon him.

The purpose of a sermon or any public speech is to drive home the point instead of the audience.

The only place one can talk in another person's sleep.

Sex

The reunifying of the originally bisexual creation called Adam . . . personality mixer . . . the most intense if not the highest pleasure . . . the cause of the curse of the population explosion . . . the prelude to the deepest calm . . . glandular gladness.

Fulton Sheen

One of the world's most versatile verbalists. A theological juggler. Better philosopher than theologian. I like him.

Silence

The opposite of children. Both creative and killing, one never knows which.

The guilty man's hell; the saint's paradise.

Very rare, heard by very few.

Exceedingly dangerous, has driven many from the wilderness to seek peace in the anonymity of the noise of the city.

Both the cause and the cure of insanity.

Sin

One of the causes of a lack of interest in church worship services is a misinterpretation of sin.

Too many ministers have assumed that sin is not really much fun—therefore, it doesn't require interesting and motivating worship services to out pull the appeal of evil.

Let's face it: if evil is a great deal of fun and Christianity is presented as a series of negative rules, the masses are going where the kicks are. There is a real giant kick in Christianity, but few of us can convey it.

Sleeplessness

Extremely valuable. More great ideas have been born after midnight than before. People should sleep during the mid afternoon. Absolutely nothing of any value has happened then. The Spanish know this. Why doesn't the rest of the world wake up and go to sleep?

Insomnia is a gift of God. During this time the nation's prophets, in restless rumination, have wrought righteousness and rugged reforms.

The need of our time is not peace of mind but troubled minds.

A nation's vitality depends on how many restless spirits there are in it.

Slums

Some areas disintegrate in a hurry evolving from e*lite* to po*lite* to red *light*.

Smoking

When one smokes, he doesn't smoke—he is just a sucker. The filters are so long on cigarettes these days that you need not worry about cancer—just that you might get a hernia from puffing so hard.

Sam Snead

I was on the putting green with Sam Snead in Palm Beach and he told me this story: Gary Player's pastor watched Gary play in a tournament. Just before the tournament began, Gary asked his pastor to pray for him as he played. The pastor agreed to do this. Player four putted the seventh hole, dropping him out of contention. Leaving the greens from the scene of the crime, Player chided his minister, "I thought you were praying for me. Where was the Lord on that last hole?"

The minister looked at his watch and blandly replied, "It's twelve thirty, Gary. The Lord is out to lunch."

Snobs

The Sacred Sorority for Snubbing Sinners.

Socialism

The discovery by the masses that they can vote government support for the lazy by punishing the creative. An extreme socialism is more dangerous to our nation's security than Communism. It makes a little more sense and is somewhat easier to sell. It is a long road to destruction. A proper understanding of this is a key to interpreting why the American people are becoming more and more apathetic.

Sodom and Gomorrah

If they were suburbs of Las Vegas, the citizens of that Nevada city would go there to Sunday School.

Sorrow

The day L. B. Bridgers lost his wife and children in a terrible fire, he wrote:

> There's within my heart a melody;
> Jesus whispers sweet and low,
> "Fear not, I am with thee, peace, be still,"
> In all of life's ebb and flow.

Jesus, Jesus, Jesus, Sweetest name I know,
Fills my every longing,
Keeps me singing as I go.

One of the biggest kicks I ever had to charbroil me was the day
Johnny Haggai, a paralyzed little boy friend of mine, said his first
word.

His famous preacher father, John Haggai, asked him, "You're
daddy's what?"

It took Johnny what seemed a minute to form his lips.
Finally he said it: "Buddy!"

John and I leaned on each other and wept.

Soul Winning

I preached at a banquet for the First Baptist Church of Cocoa,
Florida. The pastor of the church, Dr. James Sawyer, called my
attention to a rather handsome, unassuming gentleman seated
two tables away.

He was Col. Donald Eppert, Deputy Director of the Corps of
Engineers in the Cape Kennedy area. Col. Eppert's name had
been affixed to untold millions of dollars of government contracts.
Dr. Sawyer reported to me that Colonel Eppert stated the greatest
thrills of his life were the following and in this order:

1. Witnessing to his neighbors about Jesus Christ.
2. Leading his church in a stewardship campaign.
3. Helping put John Glenn into orbit.

There's a chap with the right set of values. He emphasizes the
matter that matters.

Stalin

When Stalin's body was removed from the Red Square in

Moscow, the Kremlin was interested in burying him in some more or less remote country, outside the Soviet Union. They finally decided that Israel would be the best place to bury the former Soviet leader. They changed their minds when an official from Jerusalem told them, "You are perfectly welcome to do this but we feel that we should tell you that here we have the highest resurrection rate in the world."

Start

The way to begin is to commence.

While it is true that many never complete what they begin, it is also true that negative thinking keeps most people from beginning their life's project.

The first victory I win each day is getting my body out of bed.

Steak

I wrestle with it in the early evening; it wrestles with me the rest of the night. The best steak I have ever eaten hasn't been cooked yet.

Stock Market

I am one of the most powerful figures in this nation. I can purchase one share of stock and stop the most bullish market in history.

I know why they call the American Stock Exchange "The Curb." I bought two shares and there I was—on the curb.

Suicide

Before you kill this person perhaps you should get acquainted. You might find him finer and superior to what you imagined. He could possibly become your friend.

The alternative to suicide is to really get to know the person you intend to eliminate. If you accept him, he will become other and better than he has been. In this fashion you have eliminated him without killing him.

This is the best way to get yourself off your hands.

Suit

They once called Billy Graham "Gabriel in Gabardine." Someone called me a "Demon in Dacron."

I often wear a seersucker suit—Sears sold it and I was the sucker.

T

T.V.

Parking lot for children.
A one eyed monster for two eyed morons.
Eye glue . . . my red retinas are crying for cool relief.

Tact

Some spell it "attack." A young minister was told that in order
not to lie, when he saw a baby, to exclaim "IS that a baby!" He
would not be evaluating the appearance of the infant and, at the
same time, would have the affection of the proud parents.

The next time he saw a newly hatched, red, wrinkled little one,
he exclaimed, "Is THAT a BABY?"

Proper emphasis is so important.

Tact

The ability to attack quietly. How to sell you a saddle while
stealing your horse . . . a cushioned brush off . . . the ability to
compliment a person without embarrasing him.

Tangent

You can't hit a home run when you are way out in left field.

Teenage Humor

A most interesting psychological study would be the evolution of teenage humor.

I have given up attempting to keep up with it and have devised a system to throw *them* off guard.

I have created a teenagese all my own. Some examples:

"Blah"—a person of no imagination, formerly called a square.

"Paddy out"—to leave

"She's clawing the wall"—reaction to a break up with a steady.

"A flat row"—a nothing

"A lop"—a fink

"Group"—one person

"Here"—there

"There"—here

"Trouble"—fun

"Fun"—trouble

"I wish I had heard it"—a solemn reaction to a very funny joke.

Speaking of the evolution of teenage humor, I'm very happy that sick humor is a thing of the past.

The elephant joke series was much healthier than the bizarre, sacrilege of the very ill and the way out.

I simply could not believe that really happy, vivacious teenagers would long put up with stuff like "I would cling to the Old Rugged Cross but I don't want to get splinters in my hand."

They didn't allow such blasphemy long life, thank God.

Of their own free will, American kids rejected it for elephants, Roy Raisen, Lizard Taylor, Mickey Pruney, the Retarded Apple, and the Lone Lemon. . . . . and, O yes, the four door grape from Grape Britain.

Teenagese

A foreign language, very difficult to learn.

It is no longer "square"—an unenlightened conformist is a "blah." When these twilight zoners want to go somewhere, they say "Let's paddy out to Benny's." When a girl is in mourning over her most recent steady crush, the word is "Don't bother her. She's clawing the wall."

I like the way the modern teenager keeps his feet firmly rooted right in the middle of the ozone.

Their method of making decisions is interesting. "Heads I go to sleep; tails I go to the movie. If it stands on edge, I study."

Their school relationship is invigorating. Joe Jones of Phoenix told me, "The teachers are afraid of the principal, the principal is afraid of the superintendent, the superintendent is afraid of the school board, the school board is afraid of the parents, the parents are afraid of the kids, and the kids aren't afraid of anybody."

Temper

A hotheaded preacher may enjoy "telling off" his people, rationalizing that this is his prophetic ministry.

There are quite a number of unemployed fire-eaters around.

And their paranoia often causes them to think they are Moses . . .

There is one similarity to the Deliverer—they are on the back side of the desert. They wait for the burning bush and end up selling insurance.

Texan

A giant of generosity . . . large lip . . . one who thinks Houston is better than Heaven . . . when soaked in water becomes instant bull . . . among the greatest people on earth.

Thievery

If a man kills one person he is a murderer. If he kills a million, he is an international hero.

If a man steals a hundred dollars he is sent to prison. If he steals a million, he is sent to congress.

If you must sin and want to escape in this life, at least make it gigantic.

Time

Four hours at the theatre is too brief.
Ninety minutes in church is too long.

Tip

Fertilizer for the outstretched palm . . . gratitude for attitude . . . what the waiter waits for . . . talcum for hand itch . . . mush money . . . dish dime . . . the only thing that can catch the waiter's eye.

Toys

The only difference between an adult and a child is the cost of his toys.

Transiency

Nomadic nobodyness—roaming rootlessness.

Tree

That which birds think people inhabit the trunk of.
A super sapling . . . earth hair.

Trouble

Three attitudes one can take: resent it, resign yourself to it, or rejoice in it like a Christian.

Trouble Makers

The key to understanding tensions in organizations and institutions is to realize that he who cannot lead and will not follow invariably obstructs.

Speaking of trouble, did you hear about the chicken that swallowed a yo-yo, and laid the same egg twenty times?

HST

History may record that he was one of our greatest presidents. But there won't be any history to record it because HST began the end of the world.

Trust

Trust God to take care of your insides. Don't always be thinking about your vital organs.

The Lord never intended for you to give management to your heart. If so, he would have put it within easy reach, like a pump handle. It is too intricate a mechanism for us to tamper with. Build its muscles through exercise, give it sufficient rest, then forget it. This applies to your kidneys, gall bladder, and colon.

You have been admonished to "give God your heart." As an apostle of good health, I say, "Give God your liver!" We need more Christian livers.

The Twist

The theology of some people reminds me of the twist: Sometimes it's here; sometimes it's there.

Two Heads

are better than one. I believe that is a correct rendering of the quotation.

I always thought it was true until I thought of the possibility of a two headed man who could get in an argument with himself and get so mad at him that he repudiates his other head and never speaks to him again.

The real tragedy could be that he would become a they instead of a he—at least until they made up.

And what if one head decided to become a lawyer and the other decided to become a physician. To whose office would they go?

U

U.N.

The U. N. has made an unusually effective contribution to international understanding. Few deny this. In all honesty I believe the good done by the thousands of missionaries exceeds that of the U. N.

Unfriendly Churches

The Lord of the loaves and fishes, the Lord of the hillside, would not be comfortable there. If I ever hear of any of our members making a person feel unwanted in our church, that day I declare war.

V

Vacation

You go on vacation to forget things. When I last went on mine and opened my suitcase I realized I had done just that.

Values

Jinny Lind, with a New Testament in hand, said, "I found that too much money took away my taste for this."
Our time renders unto Caesar the things that are God's.

Vision

Seeing that which is positive and upbuilding in the foliage which hides it from the visionless. I have been among those blind to opportunity too many times.

An illustration of my darkened sight took place one day in Brookhaven, Mississippi. Dr. Wayne Todd informed me that he was leaving his strong, good church to become the head of the Church Library Service of his denomination. Frankly, I couldn't see the wisdom of his decision. The idea of his becoming a glorified librarian was a tragic waste of a great personality—as I saw it.

Later I was stunned to hear that *Das Kapitel* had been more widely distributed throughout the world than the Bible; that Ross Coggins said in Indonesia communist books could be bought for ten cents, and equivalent American books sold for $3.00.

I had been blind. Todd was right. The world conflict is a battle for the minds of men. It is a battle of books.

Waffles

Retreaded pancakes. If I were to list my very favorite food, the food that appeals to me more than any other food, the food that satisfies my hunger pains and puts a spring in my step, this wouldn't be it.

Russell Walker

He was a simple, humble country minister all his life. When I was called upon to preach his funeral, I observed his family on the front row of the church: a son who teaches in a Christian College, a daughter who is a director of Christian Education in a church, a daughter who is the wife of a seminary professor, a son who serves the government in a position of trust, and another son who is one of the most faithful members any church could have.

When I stood before his coffin to speak, I realized I was in the presence of greatness and the words came freely: "We are conducting the graduation service of an extremely wealthy man—and, just think, he took it all with him . . . "

Wealth

The difference between a rich man and a poor man is what he cries into.

The rich cry into champagne.

The poor weep into beer.
The Christian saves money by crying into a coke.

Wife

When you've been married to her for twenty years, it will gradually dawn on you that you will never understand her.

Jonathan Winters

The most refreshing person in America since Will Rogers. I wish I could make all those funny sounds. He is quite a crowd.

Woman

Energetic enigma. God's most unique, intriguing and beautiful creation . . . the mixture of the elixir of the pixie and the sophisticate . . . the alpha and omega of morals . . . man's otherness . . . hell or happiness, God's companion in sacrificial creation.

Work

The church's vigor and tenacity in finding things for the preacher to do is enough to debilitate the United States Marine Corps.

Worry

"God does have a place for full time worriers—in the ulcer ward of the hospital," said an eighteen year old Wake Forest student, Bill Garrott.

Old but true: "Why pray when you can worry?" Unless you believe that mental fixation changes matter and spiritual forces, worry will be of no value. Learn the difference between worry and meditation. Meditation is positive, up-building. Worry is the antonym of meditation.

X

Xanthippe

The nagging wife of Socrates. No wonder he was always DOWNTOWN lecturing. She was that which made the hemlock almost nice.

Y

Young People

To feel young, watch them; to die young, try to keep up with them.

Youth Leader

A hustling, hyperthyroid heroine . . . Leon Mitchell says they must be "loving, limber, and a little looney."

Z

Zip's Grandchildren
The Home, 1985

If we are to eliminate the quite apparent hypocrisy of the time, the first step should be to eliminate the idea of the home.

Let the newborn child be brought into the world at one of our official human hatcheries which men in the old days called a hospital. Today it is a modern, architecturally sterile building that is called by a number instead of a name. When men were less democratic, they called it by some name—like "Good Samaritan Hospital" but, since it was a hospital for *all* the people—and some of the people were offended by a title from the Bible and the fact that it reflected a kind of sickening warmth of such outmoded concepts as compassion and neighborliness—"they" decided to call it by a number, since numbers are almost completely non-controversial (though I am told there is a growing minority who take offense at numbers three and seven.)

Since a woman has already made some significant sacrifices to bring the infant into the world, and should return to unfettered living, the newborn Homosapien can be transferred to one of our National Nurseries. There state trained infantologists can give more excellent supervision to a child than the female producer of the pygmy primate.

Such a program will put no limitations on the personality development of the female, thus allowing her to return almost immediately to her interests—under the supervision of her area director of recreation and instruction, of course.

The child will lose the necessity of feeling a need for home and will develop a sense of allegiance to the government controlled agency appointed to care for him, at his varying stages of development.

All songs, poems, and stories relating to the concept of home can be eliminated. Instead of singing "Home, Sweet Home," they can be trained to sing in unison, without harmony, "28094, Sweet 28094." The only way the child will get individual attention in school is to bend his IBM card.

When the child enters athletic contests, he can learn teamwork without frustration due to the new policy concerning excellence in sports. An outstanding quarterback will be benched and replaced by a more blended, average teammate. This will assure the team that no player will develop fixation on superiority and all will feel a sense of being a representative part of the squad. All games will end in a tie, with no scores announced.

Really now, how would it look to carry the results of a football game which would indicate the superiority of one team over another?

Imagine reading the *State News* sports page: "28694 smothers 59610—21–0!" Such would be completely eradicated.

The coaches will never be under pressure from the alumni. The image of the ulcer ridden frustrate pacing in front of impressionable youth on the bench will be erased (think of the nervous quarterback). It might develop that the players could study while waiting their turn on the playing field. Naturally, all get to play.

The crowds will be taught to cheer only when cheering for both sides, most of such displays of emotion will be limited to pre game cheering. Variety in every field will be most odious. The child will be taught religion without specifics. Absolutely nothing controversial will be allowed. All the churches will be blended on the basis of the lowest common denominator of belief. Arnold Roth would call it the *"Church of the Obscure."*

"The Church of the Obscure" will always have buildings exactly alike: no religious symbols will be allowed, lest they offend. The ministers, state trained, will be gray men in gray suits wearing a contented countenance. They will be most adroit at avoiding controversy. Their sermons will follow the line of that great theologian and apostle of happiness, Reverend Doctor Little Jack Horner of "What a good boy am I" fame.

Zzzzzz

This will assure this being the last story in my alphabetically arranged book. Also you may use as many of the Zzzzzzs as you wish if you are asleep by now.

I desire to leave you edified and not mortified, so I will close with a touching story.

Once there was a man named Zzzzzz. You pronounce that Zzzzzz. He loved to smoke his pipe and the day he was flying from West Palm Beach to New York was no exception. He got on board the jet liner, pipe in mouth. Of course, this is not allowed. Also there was a lady, a Miss Yyyy from Wyoming who brought her cat on board. This also was not permissible.

No sooner had the plane become airborne, than she protested to Mr. Zzzzzz that his pipe was disturbing her cat and besides pipes are not permitted on airplanes. He countered by letting her know in no unclear trumpet blasts that she was violating regulations by bringing the cat on board! So, Zzzzzz and Yyyy tossed the cat and the pipe out the plane.

When the plane arrived at Kennedy, do you know what they found clinging to the tail of the plane? The cat.

And you know what was in his mouth, don't you? You're right! Mr. Aardvark's brick.